THE DEATH AND RESURRECTION
OF THE CHURCH

THE DEATH
AND RESURRECTION
OF THE CHURCH

by
LESLIE PAUL

HODDER AND STOUGHTON

Copyright © 1968 by Leslie Paul

First printed 1968

SBN 340 04498 5

Printed in Great Britain
for Hodder and Stoughton Limited,
St. Paul's House, Warwick Lane, London, E.C.4,
by Richard Clay (The Chaucer Press), Ltd.,
Bungay, Suffolk

To my colleague and friend
Gordon Davies

ACKNOWLEDGMENTS

I wish to make acknowledgments to the following authors and publishers for permission to quote: to the S.C.M. Press Ltd. and the following authors: Dr. John Robinson, *Honest to God* and *The New Reformation*; Dr. David Martin, *A Sociology of English Religion*; Professor J. G. Davies, *Worship and Mission*; to Collins and Professor Ronald Gregor Smith, *Secular Christianity*; to Darton, Longman and Todd and Professor Peter Hinchliff, *The One-sided Reciprocity*; to the Editor of *The Church Times* and Canon Pawley for *The Church Times* article of 21 April 1967, 'French Bishops' Reforming Zeal'; and to Miss Jean Nutter and Mrs. Ruth Mackenzie for all their care in typing and checking.

PREFACE

The 10th Lambeth Conference, drawing some five hundred bishops of the Anglican communion from all parts of the globe, observers from many churches and scores of theological experts, has taken to itself the theme, 'The Renewal of the Church', which it will discuss under three aspects, 'The Renewal of the Church in Faith', 'The Renewal of the Church in Ministry', 'The Renewal of the Church in Unity'.

It is a timely enterprise. Churches throughout the western world—not Anglican churches alone—are passing through an unparalleled ferment. It is not one which easily shows itself to the world at large. Drop, in England, into the cathedral or church of your choice and all seems much as it always was. There are the robed clergy, the surpliced choir, the familiar hymns, the age-old canticles and psalms, the readings from the Authorized Version. In England, at least, the beautiful churches bequeathed us by past ages, resonant with ancient religious murmurs, seem themselves a guarantee of the permanence of it all. Perhaps they are, but dwindling congregations hardly seem to promise this.

The other side of the medal is the rapidly changing world scene. From nuclear power to medicinal drugs, the pace of scientific and technological advance is such that no part of man's environment, not even his interior world, appears able to resist invasion and control. Not only the world man lives in but man himself becomes in some sense a human artefact. Where the shape of secularized societies changes so fast and the urban tensions grow, what is the role of churches built for more stable eras, eras more morally secure?

Just because the pace of change accelerates, and affects religious belief and practice more and more the self-criticism of churches mounts and priests and ministers question as never before their roles and achievements. Some of the most basic doctrines of Christianity are as rigorously rejected inside the churches as ever they were before by non-believers. We are living through an age in which 'death-of-God' theologies are propounded and the continuing existence of the church as an institution is seriously discounted. My brief study is concerned with the social, doctrinal and institutional problems raised by this ferment. It comes not only from the research, commissioned by the Church of England—*The Deployment and Payment of the Clergy*—but from such studies as those involved in *Alternatives to Christian Belief*. It is therefore inevitably directed to the Lambeth Conference themes, but mostly as they are reflected in the English scene, and I hope it will contribute to the ongoing debate the historic conference must surely initiate.

Two chapters of the work have previously been published. Chapter Six, 'The Institutional and the Charismatic Church', is mostly the enlarged version of an address delivered to The World Council of Churches consultation 'The Christian Attitude to Money' at Bossey, Switzerland, August–September 1965 and published in *Laity* 21, April 1966, under the title 'The Church as an Institution—Necessities and Dangers'. Under the same title the enlarged and revised version was published in *Journal of Ecumenical Studies*, Vol. 4, No. 2, Spring 1967, and as Prism Pamphlet No. 35 under the title 'The Church as an Institution'. A large part of Chapter Seven, 'The God-shaped Blank', was first given as my Presidential Address to the Birmingham University Theological Society in October 1966 and published in a shortened form in *The Expository Times*, Vol. LXXIX, No. 3, December 1967, under the title 'The New Theology and the Idea of Transcendence'. To the editors and publishers of these journals and pamphlets I give my grateful acknowledgment. The themes of the book in general were presented in a course of ten lectures entitled 'Crisis for the Churches' organized by the Extra-mural department in Birmingham University in the spring of 1967.

LESLIE PAUL
The Queen's College, Birmingham

CONTENTS

CHAPTER ONE

WHAT THE CRISIS IS ABOUT

A crisis for the churches is not a new thing. Crises, if not perennial, are endemic. A century ago, at the time of the great Darwinian debate about evolution, the Christian churches received a moral shock as great as that of the Reformation. The biblical account of the Creation was shown to be fallible. In the aftermath of Darwin and Huxley all thinking people had to accept that immense vistas of human and geological time preceded the birth of Christ. The world was infinitely older than Bishop Ussher's six thousand years and the universe more immense than man had dreamed of. The earth was a dim speck in a wilderness of empty space. The close, caring relation between God and his creatures which the Bible proclaimed no longer appeared tenable if the evolutionary struggle was true. It could be argued that man and his societies had come up the ruthless not the loving way.

Nevertheless, the churches showed remarkable resilience, and even continued to grow. The 'eighties were a period of religious revival in Britain. It was seen that certain biblical statements made more sense as mythology than as claims to literal truth, and it was felt, often inarticulately, that religion spoke to a dimension of human experience, an area of human need, that nothing else attended to. Christian philosophers were often in the van of those earnestly seeking to relate evolution to human history and to make sense of it metaphysically. Besides, the nineteenth century was glorious with optimism about progress, and evolution seemed to make progress inevitable. Indeed, the idea of progress proved a useful bridge between faith and evolution. Progress was easily to be conceived of as God's plan for man working itself out in history. Perhaps evolution was that too.

The churches in Britain, and the Christian faith itself, received a second blow in the Great War of 1914–18. But this was a social, not an intellectual blow, and less easy to understand and to counter. One might speak of it as *a social revelation* to the Church of England. Britain raised and equipped immense proletarian armies, at first on a voluntary basis and then by conscription. These men were not the professional Tommy Atkinses of Kipling's famous poem: 'For it's Tommy this, an' Tommy that, an' "Chuck him out, the brute!"/But it's "Saviour of 'is country" when the guns begin to shoot'—social outcasts only welcome in time of war—they were millworkers, steelworkers, miners, clerks, labourers, nail makers, shop boys, barmen, tram drivers—men drawn from the apparently inexhaustible reservoir of manpower in our great industrial cities: certainly they were not the ploughboy armies of a century earlier. They fought with bravery and dogged endurance a long and hopeless war of attrition, much of it from foul and waterlogged trenches. Looking back, it is a marvel how little they protested, how great their patriotism under butchering generals. Mostly through its chaplains, the Church of England discovered with a shock its almost total estrangement from these industrial masses, and their suspicion of a church completely identifiable with the ruling classes. William Temple's National Mission of Repentance and Hope was born out of the dismay of that discovery. Typically, though, it was run from London's West End and not from the Bullring, Birmingham.

The church in its rural sleep

It would be wrong to describe the Church of England in 1914 as totally rural. Nevertheless, it was deeply rural. Many great efforts had been made from Bishop Bloomfield's reforms onward to cater for the masses in the industrial towns. Not with much success—it was the Salvation Army, not the Church of England, which in the nineteenth century broke into industrial slums and made an impression there, and shocked the nation.[1] Siegfried Sassoon brilliantly portrayed the paternalistic Edwardian rural England in *Memoirs of a Fox-Hunting Man*, an England of fine country houses and rich county families which might have stepped straight out of the pages of *Mansfield Park*—in which hunting and cricket were passions, labourers wore smocks and doffed their caps, the motor car had hardly penetrated or income tax disturbed. This was the place where most parsons were securely bedded down. It was not simply that this was where they lived. It was where they thought they ought to live, like Parson Colwood.[2] The whole ethos of the times was that country life was the right kind of life which everyone of any consequence as a matter of course wanted to live and that the industrial areas were monstrosities, aberrations, and cities in general only tolerable at certain seasons or for certain tasks or for certain people—*trades* people. Even the suburban villa growth of the period emphasized the belief that though you lived in a town you ought to make it as much like the country as possible. The country squire has been described as the permanent English ideal of manhood. The Georgian poets with their passion for country walks and week-end cottages celebrated a static rural peace—

> Stands the Church clock at ten to three?
> And is there honey still for tea?

and Harold Monro, in praise of the 'Week-End'—

> The train! The twelve o'clock for paradise.
> Hurry, or it will try to creep away.
> Out in the country everyone is wise:
> We can be only wise on Saturday.
> There you are waiting, little friendly house...

spoke nostalgically for a national mood, a national illusion that England was still nothing more than a charming rural island, outside the boring town.

It was a church unaware that it had any rural illusions which discovered the industrial masses in their military khaki between 1914 and 1918 and was alarmed by the spectacle of them as the outcast, unwanted and *red* unemployed in the interwar years. It was a baptism of shame for sensitive Christians, and the whole period of William Temple's spiritual ascendancy over the Church of England (and over other Christian bodies)—roughly from 1914 to 1944—can be viewed as a single campaign under his leadership to bring the Church to recognize the challenge of that social revelation in every phase of its life, including its government. One could not be Christian and not care, was Temple's theme.

After 1944 its leadership, drawn always from that class in England most remote from industrial life, gave up the Temple campaign. It was difficult to see how precisely, at the end of the Second World War, it could be continued. Britain emerged a more equal country from a fight which, though it exhausted her, had not plunged her into the spiritual despairs of the First

World War. The social programme of the first Labour Government was massively equalitarian. The Beveridge Report (a product of the wartime national government) led to the birth of the
welfare state and of the full employment society, to social
policies which in fact have dominated all postwar governments
and reversed entirely the governmental laissez-faire of the
'twenties and 'thirties. What was left for the church to do?

Looking back to that immediate postwar period, it now does
seem a peculiarly colourless one, despite the strenuous policies
of social renewal. Minds were still fixed on the causes for which
the war had been fought, on the mopping-up operations, on the
atom bomb and the hydrogen bomb, on the cold war which
threatened the world with a new and even vaster conflict. There
was a kind of numbness, reflected in the curious static quality of
governments (Stalin, Eisenhower, Macmillan), and in the long
continuation of wartime rationing. A state of suspended anima-
tion was true of the churches in Britain and America. A brief
postwar religious revival in Britain warmed church leaders with
the hope that men had learned the lesson of the world's capacity
for evil and were ready to return to the fold. But it was lay
voices which bore the burden of the religious debate then—one
thinks of C. S. Lewis, T. S. Eliot, Simone Weil, Maurice Reckitt
—and only unofficial organizations such as Christian Action
kept up a display of social and political militancy worthy of
William Temple.

The present storm

It was in the 'sixties that the new religious storm broke. As we
move towards the end of the decade and some of the fog clears,
we can see more clearly what has been happening and not
simply to the churches in England but to Christians the world
over. Elements in the storm have been such events as the growth
of a world-wide ecumenism, of the foundation of indigenous
churches where colonial powers moved out, the appearance of
the new theology and a new Christian radicalism and the extraordinary pressures which the birth of a new kind of society—
a mass society and an affluent society—have generated, which
bear explosively upon every social institution. Perhaps most of
all upon the churches, which are not empirical and pragmatic
organizations with limited ends but institutions rooted in ancient history and directed to divine purposes, and not readily

adaptable to social changes. There are many strands, however, not the least the breaking of the monolithic structure of the Roman Catholic church: through Vatican Two it has moved towards a free, modernized federal structure. Seen in retrospect, Pope John XXIII's enthronement in 1958 humanized and—dare we say it?—re-Christianized the oldest Christian institution. Instead of a remote, absolute monarch, surrounded with an impenetrable aura of sacredness, the world was presented with a jolly peasant priest on the papal throne who was distressed if gardeners knelt to him and could joke about a woman's *décolleté* and thought of his office as the means of an outflow of humbleness and love. A simplicity of heart almost Galilean woke his astonished church to its Gospel roots.

The other elements in the new situation are so diverse as to defy classification—the revival of interest in Bonhoeffer's wartime back-to-the-wall Christianity, John Robinson's *Honest to God*, Bishop Pike's trial for heresy in the United States, Charles Davis's resignation from the Roman Church, the Nottingham Conference on Faith and Order which has set 1980 as the date for reunion, the Keele Evangelical Conference of 1967, my own explosive Report and those it set in train[3] and the associated build-up of sociological material about religion,[4] and above all a spate of works of popular and academic theology of unprecedented thoroughness and brilliance which have put religion repeatedly in the best-seller lists. It adds up to a new ferment, not this time over evolutionary theory and Genesis, or over the relevance of the social gospel, but over something deeper than either, deeper even than the Reformation, which was a crisis over doctrinal interpretation of the scriptures, and church rule, rather than over the foundations of the faith. This is in fact an inner crisis, a crisis of the faith's foundations: it is a time of the shaking of the foundations, to borrow Tillich's title. It has to do with *secularization*, which is not only a theory about what is happening to human society but in some hands a doctrine about what *ought to happen* to the Christian faith. It is a crisis over the dechristianization of the West in the sense of its religious behaviour as well as of its beliefs, and over the struggle for a simpler and more relevant Christian presence in the world. It has the appearance already of a revolution which is going to be total. One must speak of it as *the crisis in depth*, over therefore death or resurrection for the Christian faith.

Areas of crisis and concern

There seem to be four areas of crisis or concern which invite attention, and they overlap. The first is the crisis over the understanding of the church, whether by believers or non-believers. Down the centuries the churches regarded it as their principal task to organize and to teach their followers. They brought them to worship, mostly on Sundays, the sacred day, baptized them, confirmed them, enrolled them in societies and classes and sought their money, taught their children, often in denominational schools. They separated the faithful from the rest, made them recognizable to each other and sometimes recognizable to the whole world by dress, or speech or other customs. At least one sect was prepared to call itself 'the peculiar people'. And every great church built buildings, often very beautiful, created exquisite liturgies, recruited and trained a professional ministry, distinctively clad, to guard and prop-agate its doctrines and to cherish its faithful in the high con-sciousness of being the instrument of Jesus in the world—a supernatural agency therefore, which brought both redemption and the judgment of God into this world. Great churches like the Church of Rome, the Orthodox Church, the Church of England, sought to be universal. At their height they claimed the right to be the monopolistic spiritual governors of the societies in which they were at work, setting not only the standards of worldly and family behaviour but of political life too. They were great civilizers. There was, when issues seemed simpler, a clear conflict between churches which sought this authority and denominations which wanted freedom to go their own way, on the one hand, and on the other, between Christians determined to place man, morals and society under divine judgment and secularists who rejected Christian claims as false-hood. The secularists now tend to say that Christian claims are not so much untrue as meaningless and that in terms of be-haviour Christians do not—or nearly always do not—differ very much from anyone else. On the other hand, there are Christians of all denominations who stand aghast before their vast, com-plicated and immobile ecclesiastical institutions not just for the reasons secularists give but because they do not believe Chris-tians should be a separate people, in need of a 'power-structure' in the world. They would de-institutionalize the church, or non-church it. Everywhere the traditional doctrine of the church as the separate people of God is under attack.

There is, coincidentally, an organizational and structural crisis in most churches. This is the second area one has to consider. It is linked sometimes with falling attendances and falling recruitment, with a drift from the churches. Yet where success in loyalties is considerable, as in America, it can still be asked whether what is being done is what organization and structure are really for. This kind of crisis can also be linked with the peculiar nature of urban civilization, which itself remoulds all institutions into the same conformist pattern. As a consequence, the structural crisis raises questions about the way society is developing. Assuming that the churches are right to go on doing what they have been immemorially doing through gospel teaching, worship and the sacraments, it can be asked, is the present-day organization the *right* kind of organization? The question bears acutely on institutional forms and the use of manpower and on the role of the laity—and for the Church of England it raises the propriety of establishment.

The third area, less of crisis than of concern, is the ecumenical front, because the churches of the world must soon move out of the area of discussion to actual decisions as to whether to unite or not. The hard decisions, in Britain, for instance, involve doctrine, organization, the nature of the sacraments, the validity of the ministries, the use of funds, the value of establishment or disestablishment. Decisions must somehow overcome the impediments of law and emotion, precedent and history. On the world scale the Anglican provinces have to decide whether to die to the world in order that the faith may live on in united, indigenous churches: the Romans have to decide not only whether their essentially medieval structure is to be updated but whether theologically they have passed the point of no return, particularly in the field of mariolatry.

The fourth area of crisis is—of course, of course!—the doctrinal one. For nearly two thousand years Christianity has lived with a certain frame of reference, which in part it drew from Judaism. Contrary to general opinion, it can be simply put. There is a real God, who is the world's creator. He exists, not as part of the world, or in the world, but in independence of the world (an independence of *being*, not an independence in space). He has a double relation to the world—first, that it is *his* world, since he created it; second, he has the continuing relation with it (or love for it) expressed by the trinitarian concepts of God the Son and God the Holy Ghost. Jesus, the incarnate Son, is the revelation of this God–world relationship. All sorts of consequences for belief and behaviour and for one's understanding of man follow from this basic doctrine. These do not concern us at this moment. The point is that the new theology and the 'death of God' theology put the whole frame of reference under question. If there is no God in independence, then what is meant by God is problematical, and what is meant by incarnation possibly nonsensical. 'Jesus, Son of God' becomes hyperbole. From theology at its most extreme we face the prospect of the dissolution of the Christian faith as received not only from the centuries but from the Gospels and Epistles; hence the phrase Christian atheism.

The challenge to central doctrine does not come unheralded. It springs from philosophical thought remote from theology and from far-reaching changes in society, changes in industry and technology and urban life, which present us with a world society altogether different in character from the local and natural societies which have preceded it. To the theological, intellectual and technological revolution, the word 'secularization' is slap-happily applied. Since the events in the intellectual world and the less precisely describable processes of society (particularly western society) underlie the ferment in the churches everywhere, it is at these that we must first look. The crisis cannot be understood apart from them.

CHAPTER TWO

THE SECULAR SOCIETY AND THE DIVINE WORLD

The confusion over secularization

The theme of secularization tremendously excites Western theologians at this moment of history. One cannot escape the word. It is used by the secularists themselves—Bryan Wilson's *Religion and the Secular Society*, for instance—and by theologians, as for example, *The Secular Meaning of the Gospel* (van Buren), *The Secular City* (Harvey Cox), *Secular Christianity* (Ronald Gregor Smith), *The Secularisation of Christianity* (E. L. Mascall) and *The Secular Promise* (Martin Jarrett-Kerr). But the theme haunts many who do not use it in titles—Gibson Winter, John Wren-Lewis, John Robinson, H. J. Blackham and a host of others.

But what do we *mean* by secularization? If we mean by it the escape of various intellectual disciplines from theology, so that their own canons of truth now determine what they say and do, then we are at the tail end of a process which began with the Renaissance. In science, the liberation from theology goes back to Francis Bacon at least, and his description of a scientific society in his novel, *The New Atlantis*, documents his secular approach. The foundation of the Royal Society in 1660, which banned disputes on theology, confirmed the new sciences in their freedom from ecclesiastical oversight. If we also mean by secularization the growth of the importance of the material world and material interests, then this is no new thing either, nor necessarily a bad thing. It is at least as old as the Industrial Revolution, which brought about the application of the new sciences to man's exploitation of natural resources. The radical theologians who speak about this are surely right in appealing to the instruction given to man in Genesis to have dominion over the earth and its creatures, though they are surely wrong in imagining that this instruction determines everything. However, if secularization also means the decline of the churches in influence and membership, then it has to be said that the meaning of 'decline' has to be radically examined, not only in the light of a widespread Christian non-attachment in Britain and Europe but also in the light of positive increases in church attendances and membership in the United States.

If we mean by secularization all these things in so far as they are true plus the rise of something new in human history—a new kind of society—then something of importance is being said which again compels the most critical scrutiny.

When a whole society is on the move, and possibly a world society at that, it is not only difficult to see what are the most important forces in the movement but also what will be the final outcome. Utopians writing at the beginning of the century might have predicted votes for women, popular universities, an end to hanging: some of them did. But they did not predict the hydrogen bomb, the race to put a man on the moon or the murder of a whole people. What we are *calling* secularization is in fact a confused, uncertain but dynamic world movement, under the influence of nationalism, ideology, science and industry, the outcome of which defies prediction, and when we stretch secularization to mean this new world process then we are (surely) giving the word a new meaning, even a weight it cannot bear. It is necessary also to insist that if we say not that this secularization is something which is happening and of which we ought to be aware but something which *ought* to happen, which Christians ought to welcome and 'get behind', adjusting their religion to its ideas and demands, then it is arguable that we are being invited to join in building up a new ideology. There is all the difference between having a clear view of history and advocating that what is happening ought to happen. It can quite easily be a moral difference. One may see a conflict between China and Russia plainly developing. It is different altogether to say 'this is a good thing' and 'we will help it to happen'. The difference between *what is* happening in secularization and *what ought* to happen is often confused by Christian secularizers.

If we mean all the meanings I have described and add them up to arrive at a total thing we call 'the secular society' we have to proceed with very great caution indeed. With a surprising naïveté some advocates of secularization expect not only a new kind of society (or say that in technology or the metropolis it is already here) but a new human consciousness, different in kind from anything before it. Of course, changes in society bring corresponding changes in social consciousness: these are important, but they can be ephemeral too. A sacrificial wartime fellowship in a nation does not survive a war, for instance. There remains a basic man who greets us across the centuries in the death of Socrates, the ambitions of Napoleon or Alexander, the grieving humanity of Abraham Lincoln, the courage of Columbus, the sweet humanity of Sir Thomas More or Gautama Buddha. The men and women of a common humanity greet us at simpler levels in the revenge of the jealous brothers on Joseph, the importuning of the Syro-Phoenician woman, the woman who touched the robe of Jesus, the vacillations of Peter after the arrest of Jesus, the widow with her mite. This common humanity, whether Greek or Jewish or Indian or British, can submit humbly to the voice of reason or surrender to despair, give vent to hatred or loose terror on its neighbours. The point of balance is a fine one and precariously held. Man is only in part, and discontinuously, a rational, mature creature. The most rational, scientific, technological age in human history has some of the most terrible crimes against humanity to its credit. *It has often, ironically, committed them rationally, scientifically, technologically.* Under 'the new consciousness', we may be sure, the old Adam is going to lurk. Under the new rationalism, old faiths may persist.

The man in the Clapham omnibus

A recent television survey, *Television and Religion*, prepared by Gallup Poll, showed that almost the whole adult population of Britain claims 'membership' of one religious denomination or another. Only 6 per cent do not, and this in an age when conformity for its own sake has no point. Society itself does not care whether you go to church or not. Even on difficult questions, such as, 'Do you believe that Christ was the Son of God, or just a man?' 64 per cent replied 'Son of God' as against 16 per cent 'just a man' and 50 per cent believed in 'life after death'. I know that the shrewd will say, 'Do those who replied in the affirmative know what they meant?' To that I would only reply that it is just as difficult for theologians to 'know what they mean' when they give similar replies: they are not therefore less sincere.

The poll put the clergyman first in the list of those who 'have the greatest influence for good in the community', and made flattering estimates of the churches' effectiveness. Many questions might be asked about the poll, but the results are not at all out of the ordinary. In the Paul Report I quoted earlier surveys which gave parallel results. And indeed, as this book was being written, Mr. P. R. May of the University of Durham published some interesting findings on 'Why Parents want Religion in School' in the March 1967 issue of *Learning for Living*. He conducted his survey in the north east of England among 3,232 parents, receiving replies from 1,730. The principal Church affiliation classed by parents was: Church of England, 57·5 per cent; Methodist, 19·5 per cent; other Protestant denominations, 6·0 per cent. Only 13 per cent claimed no denomination. No less than 26·4 per cent claimed church attendance regularly or fairly often (which confirms Dr. Martin's figure on page 53), and only 16·9 per cent said they never went. As for reasons for knowing about Christianity—'nearly 70 per cent of all respondents included religious reasons among those they offered, a surprisingly high percentage'. Sixty-two per cent said religious instruction was necessary because 'Christianity is true', 42 per cent because 'it is part of our history' and 50 per cent because 'it helps people to be good'. Religious justifications massively dominated reasons for approving daily school worship also, with community spirit a strong runner-up. It is proper to ask what is the meaning of these elements in our national culture at a time of decline in church-going and of the self-confidence of the churches? What does it mean that in a secular society people bow sincerely towards the sacred and spiritual and do nothing else about it? What does it mean that in America churches continue to grow in membership and influence and that in Russia half a century of savage persecution has failed to wipe out religion? If we do not remember these elusive but not less real elements in modern society we shall be in danger of over-simplifying the movement of history in which we are caught.[1]

These warnings, however, are directed against exaggerated and even hysterical appraisals of what is happening: there is no intention of denying that we are in the presence of profound social changes, particularly in the West, which will affect everything—which *have* affected everything—including religious life. Gibson Winter, in *The New Creation as Metropolis*, and Harvey Cox, in *The Secular City*, see emerging in our time, and as it were finally and universally, a particular form of society, one from which sacred ends are dismissed and in which temporal and material considerations dominate everything, while the disciplines are empirical and pragmatic. A metaphysical view of the universe and of man is useless for the 'this-world' direction of energies such a society implies, and so, too, is a religious view. The further one pursues the meaning of these writers, the more clearly one sees that they equate 'secular' with technological and metropolitan society in which they find qualities which sharply distinguish it from earlier societies.

The mass consumption society

What are those qualities? One useful guide I find not in these writers but in T. R. Fyvel's *Insecure Offenders*, a study of juvenile delinquency, in which he relates the breakdown in law to the breakdown of bourgeois society. The bourgeois breakdown is held to be basically an economic one in the sense that we are witnessing a switch from a scarcity society to a mass consumption society. In a scarcity society the most important people are those who *benefit* from it. Not only do they receive an abundance of the world's goods but all that flows from wealth amid poverty is theirs too for the asking—leadership of society, political power, monopoly of learning and law, the right to dictate the ethos and credos of the nation to a very great extent. Inevitably they decide, in a collective sort of way, who rises and falls and on what terms. To 'get on' in that society is to climb on to their band wagon. Galsworthy's *Forsyte Saga* illustrates the kind of conformity demanded of those who want to succeed in a scarcity milieu and the penalties exacted of those who fail.

In a mass consumption society the bourgeois do not disappear: they may even grow richer. But they lose their influence: when the mass of the population is moving into affluence with the expansion of the whole economy the difference between rich and poor is more relative than absolute. It is probably better to get a degree in electronics or to obey the shop steward in order to 'get on' than to bother about what the parson says. The mass media take over from the bourgeois élite the task of deciding what the masses do and think, and the mass media are run by specialists and experts for a mass market, not a bourgeois one. The demands of that market rather than a bourgeois moral code determine standards. Fyvel discovers in this just that decline in firm and accepted moral codes from which much delinquency has sprung. Hence too the teenage revolt against a society without values, their resort to drugs and their defiance of squares.

The instant society

Harvey Cox, looking at the movement from an American rather than a European base, sees it in technological terms. The city, not class, is the key. Society has been *transformed* by technology. It is technology which has created the vast new metropolises or conurbations of the world, and in them we are asked to acknowledge the consummation of the biblical command to man to have dominion over the world. The modern city for Cox, as for Gibson Winter perhaps, is the supreme creative act of man—a piece of eulogizing which plays down all that is destructive and megalomaniac in a great city. For Cox the cloverleaf highway junction and the switch-board are the images which convey the social, over against the physical, shape of the city. The cloverleaf suggests constant human mobility in every direction simultaneously, and the giant switch-board instant communication between all the diverse lives of the city, through electronic magic. Characteristics of the city are anonymity and choice. One can remain as anonymous as one chooses, but one's choices in girls, marriage, friends, activities, housing can be as wide theoretically as the city itself. Choices indeed are infinite. Relationships with the majority will be functional—one may never know even the name of the ticket collector or the cash girl in the supermarket or the face of the postman; but those with whom one has primary or face-to-face relationships —I-Thou relationships, in Buber's sense—are entirely within personal choice. In an organic community such as a village or small town they are prescribed by class, race, social or professional status, family, clan or even just proximity, and have to be endured however unendurable. The city liberates the individual man from all that is compulsive, confining, inescapable in his social environment. Anonymity, Harvey Cox says, serves 'for large numbers of people as the possibility of freedom in contrast to the bondage of law and convention'.

Perhaps only an American theologian, brought up in the Jeffersonian optimism of an energetic people, could be quite so naïve about anonymity. For it is anonymity that not only makes and fosters crime but also enables the criminal to escape without detection. It is anonymity which breeds the affectlessness of which, for instance, Pamela Hansford Johnson speaks in *On Iniquity*. When the bomb-doors of a mighty bomber high in the stratosphere open and a wave of destruction is released the crew do not (apparently) feel a personal responsibility for the death and devastation below, even for infants and the helpless non-combatants. There is an imaginative failure which renders them incapable of feeling. They perform impersonally an impersonal job on an unseen target.

Strangely the same holds true of our mass relations in our mass societies. So long as the 'others' stay in the anonymous mass to which we are anonymous too, we can 'hold off' personal feelings about them. Our capacity to view objectively on the T.V. screen the endless daily violence of society, the catastrophies of flood, famine, crash, wreck and war informs our minds while it kills our sensibilities.

The human consequences of mass and anonymity can be just disastrous, as the Kitty Genovese case showed. Kitty Genovese, only twenty-eight, was trailed by a man in Kew Gardens, Queens, New York, in March 1964. He attacked and slew her. At least forty persons heard her screams, and many of them must have seen her die. Not one came to her aid or called the police. One witness, asked why he did nothing, said, 'I didn't want to get involved.' Later the same year at least thirty persons ignored the cries for help of a Bronx telephone girl attacked by a rapist. Fortunately two patrolmen heard in time to go to her aid and save her life. There are all too many such cases.[2]

Let us be frank. On a sufficient scale, mass, anonymity, affectlessness can be the death of societies based on the rights of man and the doctrine of man made in the image of God.

The industrial enclave

There is a pointer to the power of the secular city in a contribution made by the Rev. Scott Paradise to a symposium by American episcopal clergy called *On the Battle Lines*. In this Scott Paradise speaks of the peculiar nature of a great industrial plant or works in a city. Somehow it is almost like a closely guarded foreign base. There are high walls, guards, internal services such as canteens, hospital and first aid units, fire-fighting units, as well as highly organized administrative and production systems. Citizens who do not work there may live under its walls for years without ever penetrating within. To get inside, as a stranger, one needs a pass, if not a passport.

Such enclaves are almost entirely self-regarding. Their disciplines are empirical and pragmatic. They have certain tasks to do—certain commodities to produce—and that is the limit of their corporate vision, apart from the need for political and economic freedom to continue to do so. Within the range of their productive intention they will show endless enterprise and zeal and devote the same ardour to discovering the best name and package for a breakfast cereal as to producing the latest rocket for a moon probe. The ultimate social or spiritual consequences of their tasks would be mostly beyond their corporate concern, though they could deeply trouble individuals caught up in them.

The maximum metropolis

Such plants proliferate in industrial areas. There are hundreds and hundreds of them. They create their own empires of ideas and attitudes, their own authoritarianism. Just their economic activities create a special climate. They demand huge resident populations from which to draw skills and labour, and ultimately to provide the demand for products. They require first class transport facilities to bring in raw materials and take away finished products. They need ports and airports and commuter services. They cannot function without the whole communications network—power, water, telephones, post, information. They need mass media to manipulate and 'pressurize' public opinion. They need to have access to research and to the findings of regional planning and administration—or to control them. Above all, they demand each other, and this is a snowball process in which they tend to *maximize* everything which comes within their influence—populations, power, urbanization, production—and each other. This is the story of Detroit or Pittsburgh or Chicago, and of Birmingham, Manchester, Liverpool, the Ruhr, Lyons, Milan. And it is primarily this technological maximization which gives the special quality to urban living today: and it is not necessary, of course, to live in an actual industrial area to discover this. The dependence of suburban and rural townships on the commodities, the power, transport and administrative services of the metropolis convert them into satellites. By this means the metropolitan *ethos* penetrates even remote rural areas, changing their consciousness, their expectations, their ambitions.[3]

In the light of all this the secular city constitutes an impressive human achievement—nevertheless, it has to be insisted, an accidental, a fortuitous one, never completely under social or political control, and the human consequences of which are even now not completely understood.

The secular city, in its uncontrolled and destructive sprawl, is in marked contrast with those cities of the past which were consciously designed to witness to human or divine glories, to Athens, Rome or Paris at their prime, for instance; or with those towns (of which so many still survive to grace the world scene) which unconsciously witnessed to a natural human piety, such as the Old City of Jerusalem, for instance, or Bruges or York.

The human zone

Another aspect of the secular city is its fragmentation into zones, which planners for hygienic and environmental reasons are forced to encourage. Heavy industry tends to be located here, light industry there: there are commercial centres and transport termini and amusement areas, recreational parks and open spaces on the outskirts, residential areas well defined by income bracket, slums and monochrome derelict areas. There are congested highways and motor roads overscoring every living area like impassable ravines. As a result of this, sociologists tend to argue that since the citizen needs all or many of these zones for a full life—he lives in one zone, works in another, takes recreation in a third, worships in a fourth, visits relations in a fifth—only *the entire area* can be considered the true *human* zone, and it is to this and not to village or suburb or town centre that his loyalty and his pride ought truly to belong. Of course, a man may form his greatest and most neighbourly attachments in the place where his home is, the natural centre not simply of his own life but of those he most dearly loves—wife, children, parents too, perhaps. But a Christian ministry limited to a few streets and a shopping centre—which is quite often all that a town parish is—can never properly see, let alone serve, the whole life of man. It cannot itself have a ministry to the human zone.

Churches under planning

There are other aspects of the cities we have to consider. Though escalating often from a random, sprawling, almost casual spread, they are increasingly becoming planned: the desire to plan and control them has become almost obsessive among city-dwellers because life without control becomes more and more intolerable, though all controls involve some infringement of human liberties. Every great city must cater not only for traffic flow, for instance, but also plan for traffic restriction and segregation before the city reaches the situation where the mechanical device which makes it so accessible destroys it as a place to live in. The computer is recruited: ultimately this means an increasing ability to anticipate the growth and needs of the future city. This has already advanced far enough for many a city not only to plan and build estates in terms of future need but also to provide for their obsolescence in thirty or forty years' time. The old sense of building houses as it were for everlasting is giving way to another mood altogether: instead of houses we may have temporary and disposable machines for living in.

This, too, must affect churches. They will have to think in terms rather of a flexible, adaptable ministry to areas whose life will be in decades rather than in centuries and in which the shape of ministry will have to be determined by fluctuating social needs and opportunities rather than dictated by an unchanging pattern of parish boundaries and 'everlasting' churches. It might well be, however, that the role of cathedrals and certain central or strategically placed churches will increase and their symbolism become more striking as points of stability, as still centres, at the hearts of cities in flux. All the same, experience already shows that the churches must not only inform themselves of planning procedures but also where they can *become party to them*, feeding information on their congregations and their needs to planners and receiving in return demographic information vital to their own effectiveness. Nor is it any longer possible to proceed in a leisurely fashion, 'booking' a church site when an estate is being planned and building after all the people have got there. The churches will be better served if they can be fully integrated with the estate or new town, building from the very beginning, and on an ecumenical basis, so that there is a Christian presence from the start to welcome people in and to provide a strong part of the motivation for the founding of a community.

How free is the anonymous citizen?

Important in the thinking of Harvey Cox is his conception of the freedom and mobility of the secular city. He hails this as a tremendous victory for progress. Anonymity is the guarantor of freedom of choice: in the secular city one is not part of an organic community which tyrannizes over one socially, something those who have experienced the bigotry of small American towns must deeply appreciate—though happily British experience is less searing in this respect. One is free of the snooper, the organizer, and (in leisure) unseen by the boss. Before we shout 'hurrah' it has to be asked—does man belong only to the community of his choice, or has he obligations, despite himself to the community of necessity? A man at his place of work belongs to a community of necessity: he may have no love for his fellow-workers, but he has inescapable obligations of loyalty and trust towards them, often more exacting and fulfilling than those of the community of choice. One can always leave the swimming club which becomes a bore, or, given modest means, move out of the ticky-tacky suburb where one is unpopular. The soldier cannot leave his company just because he does not get on with it. The parable of the good Samaritan instructs us that one's neighbour is the anonymous stranger across the road and that neighbourliness may involve steeling oneself to danger, disease, rejection, to love of the unlovable. The community of choice, pushed to the limit, is productive of the selfish-well-to-do ghetto, blind to the agony of the ghettoes of necessity where the coloured or the social rejects live: after all, just this is the great social disease of American cities. The Christian task today cannot be to oppose freedom of choice but rather to enlarge it, for we have to live still with the destructive consequences of an 'obligatory' and 'conformist' Christianity. But fulfilment *only* through community of choice could mean only complete social fragmentation as we seek to absolve ourselves from all that is unpleasant and personally unrewarding in our social relations.

Besides, the anonymous city offers its glittering prizes to the adventurous and successful. They, in a kind of way, plunder it, exploit its liberties. A law of diminishing returns from city life applies more and more poignantly as one moves across the spectrum from those fit and energetic enough to feel that the city belongs to them, to the poor, the misfits, the delinquents, the failures, the suicidal, the sick, the lonely, the old. Many of these must think of themselves as the victims of the city rather than its beneficiaries. The geriatric ward, where the abandoned old are set out in rows to die, the junkie unit and the mental hospitals, full of those shattered by the inexorable pressures of life, are equally, with the cloverleaf and the telephone exchange, symbols of the secular city. There anonymity means not only personal loneliness but also a kind of non-existence—the lonely old person in a single room is simply not 'seen' and 'belongs' nowhere and to no one. The city of those aspects is a disaster, and the organic community which almost intuitively knows itself would be an undisguised blessing. The suicidal are often saved simply by being seen and known in some face-to-face encounter with someone who cares enough to abandon his own anonymity *in order* to serve the city's casualties. It is in this spirit that the Samaritans function.

We have to remember the hard painful facts of our urban civilization. In Britain every year the *reported* suicidal attempts total about 40,000. About 5,000 of them succeed, according to Mary Holland;[4] about half the suicides are of people over sixty. About one half of all the hospital beds in the United States and Britain are occupied by mental or psychiatric patients, and about one third of all patients consulting doctors appear to be in need of psychological treatment.

There is another point. The extension of freedom of choice means the extending of options. In the city there are not four or five local activities in the evenings or at week-ends out of which one chooses one or two, as in the old, smaller communities, but an immense range of recreational activities and entertainments across the city, some demanding high degrees of skill or specialization. No citizen can encompass all, or afford all. A high degree of selectivity is called for: this means inevitably that many activities call out eclectic groups of supporters, rather than support based on pure community. The ordinary man tends to fall back on obligatory undertakings—work and family

—and warily to restrict the options he takes up beyond that to the minimum he can manage. There can be therefore a community impoverishment which everyone, for instance, trying to organize local political life becomes aware of. There is a spiritual impoverishment too when no discipline of life is called for, and nothing is of necessity except work. The church, of course, becomes one of the life options to be taken or left alone. It must compete at week-ends with the trip in the car with the kids, the statutory visit to parents, a walk in the park, mowing the lawn, painting the bathroom, the sacramental Sunday lustration of the car or that great national Sunday industry—reading the Sunday papers in bed. (Camus described modern man as one who fornicates and reads the papers.)

The churches, in such a society, easily, but unconsciously, find themselves moving to the periphery of society, where they become obsessed with the trivial. What they say and what they do no longer agitates the core of the community, but becomes the concern only of particular hot-house 'in-groups'. Then the contemporary churches no longer lead or dominate the nation. The nation turns from them and makes its moral judgments by light of the traditions of centuries, a kind of spiritual deposit from ages of faith, which some have called *civil* religion, to which somehow a doctrinal or ritualistic religion seems quite irrelevant.[5]

Secularization and Christian positivism

There are grave intellectual objections to the theoretical side of secularization, at least as it emerges in Harvey Cox's theology.

Two considerable theories of history clamour for the loyalty of Christians just now: they are Teilhard de Chardin's evolutionary doctrines on the one side, and a kind of Christian positivism on the other. Teilhard sees the whole cosmos as in the grip of a great expansive force rolling all things, including men, on towards some cosmic appointment with God. It is Bergson baptized, evolution sacralized. The opposite doctrine of *secularization* is that men are in charge and rolling away from God. It is associated with such notions as 'man's coming of age' and 'religionless Christianity', and receives a clear and honest expression in the Bishop of Woolwich's *The New Reformation*, particularly in his essay 'Can a truly contemporary person *not* be an atheist?' The elements of this doctrine I have already made familiar: man in the modern world becomes more self-reliant and responsible; he looks to his own resources and not to God's; his ways of thinking are pragmatic and functional and exclude the dimensions of the religious and metaphysical. If Christianity is to speak in that world, it is said, it must demythologize itself and strip itself of metaphysics too. It must present a purely human Christianity and never talk of that which is beyond or unknown: it is the manly sacrificial life of Jesus which is all the God we shall ever know. Van Buren has gone farthest in this secularization of Christianity.

The point remains—are we talking about the necessity of translating a basic and irreducible Christianity into the socio-cultural language of our age; or are we talking about some irreversible historical process in which Christianity itself is caught? If the former, the problem is one of communication only; if the latter, Christianity changes inexorably from age to age, and there is no longer a body of doctrine handed down by history but only what each age can do in speaking of its God-consciousness, or Christ-consciousness, if it has these things. If this process is regarded positivistically, in the true Comtean sense, then the latest stage of the process is superior to earlier ones and is the product of them: we could be argued to be in the presence therefore of a 'religious' evolution which can only go on producing superior stages. If the process seems to result in the abandonment of 'religion' and of metaphysics too in its turn and the limiting of human consciousness to technical, functional or pragmatic tasks and of society to types of social, political and technological organization which make this possible, then we are not to understand this as an amputation of human consciousness but as that which God, or Christ, or history intended—as something which liberates and advances human consciousness!

If I understand *The Secular City*, Harvey Cox is arguing precisely such a Christian positivism. It is a brilliant but erratic book, full of fine and profound insights, and no one can read it without profit. I like particularly his understanding of the fact that men in cities need impersonal functional relations if they are to serve each other and survive, and his consequent stripping down of the Buberian 'I–Thou; I–it' to size. I admire his final chapter 'To speak in a Secular Fashion of God' and agree with much of it. I dislike his descriptions of four great cities in the context of his argument: they are so brief and scrappy as to be derisory. I think his proposition that John F. Kennedy and Albert Camus are representative men of the 'technopolitan' age ludicrous: he speaks of Kennedy as the representative pragmatist and Camus as the representative of the profane. But Kennedy represented too a cultural, if not religious, protest against many aspects of his age. And Camus, good Lord, was full of a violent protest against an age which 'fornicates and reads the papers'. He would have squirmed at Harvey Cox's complacent acceptance of technopolis. But if Harvey Cox insists on his names I will put up two more—Ford and Oswald—the one the technological empire builder who created the mass-consumption society, and for whom history was bunk, the other the typical deracinated product of the great cities in whom the urban dissociation of sensibility—affectlessness—was complete.

I protest most about the building-up of Harvey Cox's theories of secularization and the growth of 'technopolis' into yet another boring doctrine of history. It is one thing altogether to try to understand our very complex and headlong age, and especially the role of vast conurbations and the secularized masses within it, but quite another to idealize and romanticize this into a God-given or history-given leap in an inevitable socio-political progress. That is to make psychologically irresistible that which perhaps ought to be resisted in many of its aspects: it was because in a utilitarian age men thought a man's individual right to do what he liked with his own was irresistible that we were landed with deserts like the industrial slums and suburbs of England and have desperately now to try to humanize them. A somewhat similar belief in irresistible rights has produced Los Angeles and New York and endless American urban sprawls which the United States is now seeking to control and humanize too, before it is absolutely too late. It seems a pity to make a God out of such witnesses to human incapacity.

Alas, Harvey Cox has worked it all out in positivistic fashion. There was, he asserts, a tribal social form with its accompanying socio-religious context—animistic and possessive about its Gods; it was followed by a town or polis form, again with its social and cultural expressions, and a religious consciousness which was largely metaphysical: today we are in the epoch of the secular city (technopolis), and it has that pragmatic and functional social consciousness to which metaphysical or earlier

B

forms of religious consciousness are meaningless. The responsibility for this directional flow of history is largely with Judaeo-Christian 'religion', the thought of which since Genesis has been directed to freeing men from dependence on God and pushing them into self-responsibility and religionlessness.

Even if this alarming simplification of history is arguable, is it, in its own terms, on the right lines? Tribes live in the most intense social consciousness of their collective life, and by a hundred devices strengthen it to preserve it from destruction: a consciousness almost as great accompanied the rise of the polis, and everything was done to beautify and glorify it. When polis-consciousness died, what succeeded it?—as intense and patriotic a love for London or New York or Tokyo? Not a bit—no citizen of these cities is ever likely to feel for them as even a non-Athenian Greek felt for Athens. These cities atomized social consciousness. *If it came to rest anywhere it was upon the belligerently self-conscious nation-states.* That is still true, though race and class consciousness too have from time to time eroded it. An explosion of nations into war could result in the total destruction of technopolis after technopolis: the reverse could not happen. On his own terms of making sense of history, Harvey Cox fails, therefore, to account for the most powerful (and mystical and sacred and far from dead under secularization!) force in contemporary history, which is nationalism.

But do we need another inevitable doctrine of history? This surely we could be spared! One thinks of so many botched up in the academies and so ruinous of human society, each containing some half-understood truth raised to a historical command for which men had to be ready to die—Marx, Spengler, Nietzsche, Rosenberg, what have you! If history itself has not taught us the danger of theories of historical determinism, then modern scholarship can do so. Harvey Cox is acutely aware of the opposition of philosophers to metaphysics: does he not know the equally solid attack of historians on metahistory? Theologically, Harvey Cox's doctrine of history is yet another way of possessing God, of knowing what his mind and intentions are in the world and social history. How vigorously he protests when others do it! How necessary it is therefore to protest to him. And perhaps it is the more necessary to protest just now, before the eminently sensible discussions of the secularized world we have all been reading harden into yet another ideology we have to live through before we can breathe fresh air again. Let us have the humility to admit that we do not know what the future holds for mankind and do not understand the present, and refrain therefore from climbing, as Christians, on to any more creaking ideological bandwagons.

I myself first read *The Secular City* at the same time as Roland Bainton's *Christian Unity and Religion in New England*[6] which constitutes the fourth volume of his *Collected Papers on Church History*. The very first essay is devoted to Harvey Cox's theme: it is entitled 'The Unity of Mankind in the Classical-Christian Tradition', and it discusses in a compressed way, but without an ideological line, the many events and ideas which contributed to a sense of cosmopolitanism in man and the fragmentation of this human dream into truculent nationalisms, each a law to itself. This he rather attributes to Machiavellianism. There's a point. Machiavelli taught the pure doctrine that power is its own justification. The secularized city, particularly in America, often seems to be a perfect expression of this doctrine. By what or by whom is it to be humanized and made to account for its power over lives? Not surely by a church which simply accepts it as the latest and best and most necessary expression of history or of God?

CHAPTER THREE

WHAT CAN THE CHURCH BE?

The world turned upside down

We do not need to accept the term secularization at its face value in order to see that the world, and not only the western world, is in the throes of immense changes. On the one side, a population expansion to which no end can be foreseen, on the other, scientific and technological progress which may, mercifully, enable the new millions arriving every year to be fed: on the one side, weapons of destruction which can bring the world to an end within a few minutes; on the other, the struggle, through the United Nations, to build a new world order: on the one side, a tendency to criticize and analyse everything in obedience to empirical and sceptical techniques; on the other, the desperate need, to which so much contemporary literature bears witness, to find an enduring basis for man's existence, a basis which sustains his dignity and his confidence in his own enterprises, and gives eternal value to his temporal loves.[1] One only has to put things in this way to see that one is speaking finally of a religious crisis in the affairs of men, the kind of crisis for which the church was called into existence. Yet the truth is that the church is itself unfitted to help because it, too, is suffering a crisis of confidence as deep as that in any other department of human affairs. One form of that crisis is the critical examination going on in all the great churches of *the church's doctrine of itself*.

The present age would seem to be the first since the Reformation in which the questions have gone so deep. But in some senses, as I have recently pointed out,[2] the questions are even more fundamental than any posed earlier.

The churches preached Jesus

Every Christian church, of course, roots itself in the New Testament story. It would regard itself as following the express commands of Jesus to his followers: 'All authority in heaven and on earth has been given to me. Go therefore and make disciples of all nations, baptizing them in the name of the

Father and of the Son and of the Holy Spirit, teaching them to observe all that I have commanded you; and lo, I am with you always, to the close of the age.' St. Matthew reports Jesus as saying this in his post-resurrection appearance to the eleven disciples on a mountain in Galilee. All the Gospels speak of the sacramental meal at the Passover: all Christians took this as the solemn ceremony which from that time forward was, however interpreted, to bind the faithful in Christ. The eucharistic wine was 'the blood of the covenant' poured out for many. John carries, in the last chapter of his Gospel, as part of the post-resurrection encounter with disciples at the lakeside, an account of Jesus' instruction to Peter, the senior disciple, to tend and 'feed my sheep'.

Taking the simplest possible view of the Gospel records (and accepting, too, that they are records edited in the light of early church experience), there can be no doubt that the prophet from Nazareth condemned to die on the cross regarded his earthly work as unfinished and entreated his followers to continue it. Even on that basis, a mission was born.

Yet no church founded itself on the precepts of Jesus as recorded in the Gospels alone. It may be put this way: Jesus preached the good news, the churches preached Jesus. They made the most radical reassessment of the whole life of Jesus in the light of the Easter events. They saw, with a conviction more passionate than any in human history, not just the good man from Nazareth done to death, but God himself in Jesus crucified but resurrected; suffering but glorious; incarnate Son, redeemer of the whole world. It was the élan of this transcendental understanding of Jesus that swept the church into proselytization outside Jewry, and changed the world. It saw itself as continuing in the world the mission of Jesus from beyond the world. Sustained by the Holy Spirit, it armed, informed and commanded the followers of Jesus. The early church therefore became quite soon a complicated rather than a simple thing, wrestling, as the Pauline epistles show, at the profoundest level with the metaphysical and doctrinal questions raised by the vehement assertion of the divinity of Jesus. It was never possible therefore to conceive of the church only as the continuation of Jesus' interrupted Palestinian mission, rather it was experienced as the living instrument of the living Jesus, and so concretely that the church was asserted to be the Body of

Christ and his followers 'members' of the Body. In the Gospels, Jesus speaks with personal authority. Inevitably this authority was held to be transferred to the church he founded as his instrument.

The struggle to comprehend as well as to preach Jesus transformed the church, which in the end preached of itself as a supernatural instrument or entity in the world, carrying the authority, the will, of Jesus, who is God, from beyond the world, bearer of 'the truth' and commanded to see that it prevails.

So argued, the claim, strengthened down the ages rather than weakened, is a staggering one, particularly as the *visible* church was at all times seen to consist of ordinary fallible men. Yet the confidence that these claims inspired made the church the breaker and maker of its world. At the very moment of the collapse of the Roman Empire St. Augustine, in *The City of God*, raised the banner of the unchanging heavenly city in the face of the crumbling temporal world. The church was the earthly representative and vehicle of that heavenly city. It swept through the West by virtue of the certainty that it was superior to any power which might oppose it.

Whatever we might be disposed to say in criticism of doctrines of the church, it was the self-confident assertion of divine rule over the world that gave us a church to be critical about, a civilization to be critical in, the sovereign intellectual individual with the audacity to be critical.

A church of love or judgment?

The resignation of Charles Davis from both the priesthood and membership of the Roman Catholic Church in December 1966 concentrated attention sharply on the doctrine of the church, at least in its Roman form. In an *Observer* article[3] Davis was trenchantly critical. 'Far from experiencing the papal authority as a living doctrinal centre,' he wrote, 'focussing and representing and sanctioning the mind of the Church, I am compelled to the admission that the Pope is enmeshed in an antiquated court system, where truth is handled politically, free discussion always suspect and doctrinal declarations won by manoeuvring.' He went on, 'The Western church was led in the course of its history to build an elaborate institutional set-up. Unhappily the Roman Church has made this structure an absolute. But that Church is now internally torn by tension and incoherence, since its institutional faith is in truth incompatible with biblical criticism and modern theology.'

He found a sharp contrast, in the Report of the Second Vatican Council on the Constitution of the Church, between the biblical theology of the church and the exposition of the doctrine of the institutionalized church with its fossilized feudalism and its 'obsessive concern to preserve papal power intact'. He could no longer believe in the official church 'as the mode of Christian presence in the world'.

We see what Davis means by the feudalism of Rome. Indeed, imperialism would be a better term, since onwards from Constantine the church took on itself an imperial form and the pope became *pontifex maximus* rather than supreme lover of suffering mankind. Institutionally, love was subordinated to judgment.

There was a touch of inevitability about this. The doctrine of the church already discussed asserts the regency of the church on earth. It has the keys. It can bind and unbind. It has authority in heaven. The special doctrine of the papacy makes the pope the inheritor of the authority of Peter, to whom expressly Christ granted plenary powers. If not only the regency of the church but the regency of the pope over the church is accepted, then the authority of the pope, even in an imperial sense, is hardly in question. Then, inevitably, we invite something feudal and imperial to grow in Roman Catholicism— authority flows down from Christ to pope, to church, to people: duty and obedience are owed upward from laity to church to pope to Christ. The question is—is this Roman Imperial pattern biblical? It is arguably biblical if one looks to Jesus and no further for a mandate to exercise authority. It is non-biblical if one asks whether the living mission of Jesus and his sacrificial passion, rather than his occasional authoritarian instructions, set out the earthly pattern the church must follow. The one set leads to political and moral authoritarianism, the other to the humility of the suffering servant, for whom truth rather than power is the supreme good. If one looks back to the issue—the sale of indulgences to pay for the building of St. Peter's—which sparked off the Reformation—one sees the juridical conception of the church clearly manifested. The church with powers to loose or bind could shorten or lengthen

the time spent in purgatory. In the medieval expression of the
church its Dantean powers seemed the most important of its
functions. But ability to submit men to the terrors of hell seems
to us today totally at odds with the spirit of love and humility
which generally characterized the Palestinian mission of Jesus.

Protestantism and the form of the church

Of course, the imperial doctrine of the church was ques-
tioned. Protestants rejected the form of the church. They asked
for congregational or presbyterian authority; for the right to
call ministers to, and out of, their congregations; for an ecclesiastical organization in which neither pope nor bishop stood
between a minister and God; for biblical rather than institutional loyalty; for the desacralization of the ministry; for the
supremacy of individual conscience. The papal proclamation of
the authority of Peter was argued to be based upon a useful
misreading of the Scriptures, and the Roman Catholic claim to
be the sole legitimate Christian presence in the world was hotly
contested to the point, in the Reformation at least, where Rome
was angrily accused of being the usurper, the predicted anti-
Christ.

The authority of Rome was contested legally and politically
by the secular powers also. The Roman church as an autonomous juridico-political system owing allegiance to an external
pontiff, the pope, had to face continuous secular resistance. The
best example of this struggle is in the emergence of a separated
Church of England in the sixteenth century. In the England
which preceded the reformation of Henry VIII we can trace
two separate systems of power. On the one side, the ecclesiastical with its properties, orders, laws, courts and final papal
allegiance, and on the other the courts, magistrates, systems of
military obligation, Parliament, rising up to the King's power.
Whether the secular had authority over the spiritual generated
the conflict which brought Beckett's and More's martyrdom
and Henry VIII's Act of Supremacy. Although in theory the
Act made the king ruler of both independent systems, in fact it
was the king-in-parliament, or the king-with-parliament, which
held the supreme power.[4] In the end it was not the king alone
who ruled over convocations, but Parliament too, and when
Parliament became supreme and the monarchy a mere device,
it led to the inevitable subjugation of the Church of England

to the secular arm. This subjection continues down to our own day: from equality with the secular the church has shrunk to the dependence of a minor department of state. This is the *de facto* secular answer—made in one way or another the whole western world over—to the original juridico-political claims of Rome. It illustrates what Charles Davis puts in question—whether the juridico-political structure (which the Church of England pathetically parodies) is the proper Christian presence in the world. Is the church to have the form of an imperial state, or the looser structure of the Palestinian mission, or if this is too bare an antithesis, can the question be posed this way—which *ethos* should inform its organizations? The Palestinian or the imperial, the suffering or the authoritarian?

The supernatural church

The fact remains that the churches which hived off from Rome or were established in opposition to her had still a common view of their tasks. They had to preach the risen Christ, to celebrate the sacraments, to cherish and discipline their flocks. They established sacred buildings, their ministries were as sacred (though not necessarily as priestly) as the Roman priesthood, their sacred scriptures were the same as Rome's, their prayers and needs close, their authority over their followers was as strong as, or stronger than, Rome's. In Calvinism the juridico-political claim appeared in a new guise. Protestantism was the Roman pattern with variations, even down to the parish. Nonconformism, it might be said, was as authoritarian as Rome, but bourgeois rather than feudal in form. A different view was taken of authority; it might rest in a confessional statement—a contract!—rather than in an institutionalized person. And so the Christian churches have continued down to our own day to draw their members into sacred buildings, principally on Sundays, to hear the Gospel preached, to pray and to praise God, and otherwise to celebrate their gatheredness. They have done this under the authority and leadership of ministerial élites with power over doctrine—and for whom 'apartness' was claimed—and under the assumption that this was their principal service to God.

There was an utter certainty behind all this of a basic division between the sacred and the secular, of the impermanence, even the futility of the secular, of the ultimate and everlasting triumph of the sacred realm, to which Christians finally belonged, beyond the grave. It is the theme of great Christian classics—Dante's *Divine Comedy*, Milton's *Paradise Lost* and *Paradise Regained*, Bunyan's *Pilgrim's Progress*. But it is also significant that at this moment of history we have constantly to remind ourselves of this powerful other-worldly element of Christianity. The sense of an immortal destiny for man has been imaginatively if not theoretically lost. There has been over the years, but accelerating in our time, a stripping bare—first the devil, then hell, now heaven; first the divinity of Jesus, then the existence of God. The effect of the new theology and of the doctrine of secularization upon the church's understanding of itself is profound.

The supernatural under attack

I have spoken of the church as a supernatural power operating in the natural world. If this is foundational, then it is easy to see how the central doctrine of the church is threatened by the new theology.

In Dr. Robinson's theology (in *Honest to God* and elsewhere) the supernatural (or as he calls it, the 'supranatural') is the direct target of attack. There is no other-worldly God at some 'distance' from this, a 'being' with a 'place' or heaven of his own. This God from outer space is a myth—no more therefore than a metaphor, a poetic image, a Father Christmas story. Dr. Robinson retains a confused sense of God as 'depth' or 'ground' of being and of the significance of Jesus as the perfect embodiment of love, and as 'the man for others'. All the same, the divinely willed church founded on the miracle of the resurrection seems to go. The church remains as an institution of course, as a 'do-gooder' in a harsh world, but it is stripped of supernatural power, of divine mandate. Whatever finally comes out clearly as the basis of Dr. Robinson's theology, a new doctrine of the church will be required of those who accept it.

Dr. Robinson retains a sense of the numinous God. His Christ is still in some peculiar way a sacral Being. Paul van Buren, in his influential *The Secular Meaning of the Gospel*, strips away every element of the sacred. It is possible to interpret everything, he argues, in a secular, a this-worldly fashion. God is semantically dismissed and Jesus retains his stature only as the man of freedom whose freedom was infectious enough to inspire his followers to continue his mission after his death on the cross. By such an interpretation of Christian origins, the church becomes at best a society of men loving Jesus but with no more authority in the world than their record of human works and moral behaviour would entitle them to.

Both these theologians have been deeply influenced by theories of secularization: both are seeking to adjust, or make over, the church in the light of the triumphs of secularization in a world 'come of age'.

It is Harvey Cox's theme in *The Secular City*, as has already been described; there he develops his own theory of the church. He argues that the church must be judged by irreversible processes in history and society rather than by its own transcendental claims. He develops two themes. The first, as I have shown, argues that the metropolis is a turning-point in human history, involving an absolute change in ways of life and human consciousness, and it will therefore destroy or transform churches along with all other organizations based on outmoded forms of consciousness and society. The second is that in this irresistible movement towards secularization, towards an autonomous scientific and technological society, the Judaeo-Christian religion has been a leader, weaning man from superstition and reliance upon the supernatural to complete self-dependence: it is, in fact, a secularizing religion.

It follows that Harvey Cox has a role for the church. It is to be 'God's avant-garde' and 'cultural exorcist'. It is not for him in the first instance an institution, 'it is a people'. The role of this people should be to create institutions which enable them 'to participate in God's action in the world'. But this action, let us be clear, could be argued to be diametrically opposed to the imperial model of the church. It would be the task of liberating man to freedom and responsibility, not of judging him. At the same time 'personal freedom and responsibility' might also be shown to be out of tune with the spirit of the Palestinian mission, with its sombre note, 'Repent ye', and its demand for submission to the will of God. Harvey Cox speaks of the church's kerygmatic, diakonic and koinoniac functions (one has to apologize for this maniac theological jargon). The kerygmatic function is to broadcast the seizure of (worldly) power. The revolution which Judaeo-Christianity began is just about accomplished. Man not only should but now *can* 'have dominion over the earth'. Let the church then ring the bells of heaven to proclaim the coming of this kingdom of technological rule! The diakonic function is to heal the 'urban fractures' and produce the true human zone, the reconciled metropolis. The koinoniac function is to make visible the city of man—'wherever cogent and tangible demonstrations of the City of Man appear today, these are the signs of the kingdom'. In the role of 'cultural exorcist', for which Cox also casts the church, he expects it to function as a healer, casting out neuroses. The particular fields in which it ought so to serve are urban strife, work and play, sex, the universities and religious life. It must cast out 'the mythical meanings that obscure the realities of life and hinder human action'.

It is entirely a humanist, 'this-worldly' programme of action, quite suitable, stripped of the justifying jargon, for an advanced, idealistic political movement. Indeed, the model Cox has chosen for the church is obviously the American Freedom movement. For him (not unfairly) the struggle for Negro rights, for racial integration, is Christianity set down in the market place and on the barricades.

The authority of a secularized Christianity

One has to ask, on what authority does a *secularized* Christianity undertake these social and political tasks? In view of the confusing mythical lumber it carries and Cox complains about, the moment of its almost-triumph ought to be the moment of its dissolution, so that less encumbered, more pragmatic agencies, might take over. If, on the other hand, it is believed that the church has a divine mandate from God, or a quasi-divine mandate from Jesus, then it has to be asserted that neither mandate was ever purely a 'this-worldly' mandate. Neither Jesus nor his church was happy about purely worldly successes. The world, ruled not only by technology but also by time, by suffering, by failure, by death, was one in which no triumph was ever a permanent one. It was the Christian assertion of triumph over the world *through triumph over death* which made the church what it was: necessarily, that triumph was 'other-worldly'. If Cox denies the 'other-worldly' element of the Christian religion, then it is difficult to see by what authority the church is mandated to perform the tasks he asks of it or in what sense it is an *indispensable* agent. If the 'other-worldly' element is not denied, then Christian judgment has also to fall on the world we are commanded to praise. That Christian judgment has always been that the world is not all: it is not self-sufficient, and man's loyalties cannot be to the world alone.

What is the proper Christian presence?

We see, then, the depth of the crisis. The kind of attack made by Charles Davis on the Roman Church places *the institutional forms* of the churches under question. If they are juridico-political, imperial or authoritarian, are they the proper Christian presence in the world in this age? The question carries another—has the church ever really reconciled its doctrine of itself as a supernatural instrument in a natural world, possessing the keys of heaven and hell, with the humiliated role of Jesus in his Palestinian mission?

The kind of attack made by Harvey Cox, on the other hand, crystallizing much of the thinking about the church by new theologians, is directed against *the spirit of Christian mission*. The task of churches is not to withdraw themselves from the world, not to create holy huddles, spiritual ghettoes, in the world. It is not their job to preach the *other* world and to denigrate this. It is their task to engage themselves as fiercely as possible in society at every growing point, with every movement of advance in liberation: in this they would bring to this century the tempo, the élan of the Palestinian mission of the first century. This demand inevitably calls all the traditional tasks of Christian churches which separate men from society under question, even separate worship, prayer and withdrawal as a special people. It is even more radical than Charles Davis's criticism. It would seem to me not to place *the institutional forms* of the church only under attack, but to dispose of the *raison d'être* of *a Christian existence*.

We know that all these critiques of the church's doctrine of itself spring in part from rapid and extraordinary changes in our western civilization. Yet once the critiques have been formulated, they acquire an existence of their own. The church has then to face not only the changes themselves but—mixing my metaphors—a battery of criticisms from within. Of course, the criticisms arrive at contradictory verdicts. The result can be destructive unless, following Toynbee's theory of 'challenge and response', the vitality of the response is of the same order as the ferocity of the attacks. Have the churches, spiritually and organizationally, and looking to God, the power of recovery and readjustment the situation demands?

CHAPTER FOUR

CHANGING SOCIETY AND CHANGING THE CHURCH

The prognosis of decline

One way to discover whether the churches are in a position to meet the challenge of this century with a living and effective response is to look at their *actual* situations as against their theoretical or doctrinal ones. This I shall do in the next three chapters, looking principally at the Church of England, which, of course, I know best.

Here our first consideration must be whether, *even by traditional standards*, the Church of England is doing the job it claims and expects to do.

In Church Assembly of July 1960 Lt.-Colonel Madge of Winchester rose and moved a resolution, deceptively simple in its terms, asking for an enquiry 'in the light of changing circumstances' into 'the system of the payment and deployment of the clergy' which would result in recommendations to Church Assembly. The resolution, which was passed, was amended to give the (then) Central Advisory Committee for the Ministry charge of the enquiry.

The date of the debate is important. The 'fifties were over. England was becoming an affluent society, but not a more religious one. Many faithful church people, like the mover of the resolution, felt that the postwar opportunity to modernize the church had been lost and that the dust was settling on the antiquated machinery again. The prewar and wartime manifestoes for the reform of the church, such as Canon Demant's *Thy Household the Church* with its almost angry demands for reform, and the more remarkable wartime *Putting Our House in Order*—signed by no less than thirty-six bishops and a great company of clerics and laymen, making recommendations about the parson's freehold and stipends not dissimilar to those I was to make in my Report, had been forgotten. There was a sense that the church, after the vigorous Temple era, was sliding back into the eighteenth century.

47

Concern was shown in the debate over the bad use of expensively trained manpower, which prevented the church from doing its pastoral and mission work properly, and the creaking stipendiary machinery, not only cumbersome and absurd in itself but also hindering the payment of a living wage to parsons and curates. Above all, the challenge the new century was making was being missed, it was felt.

The report I made, *The Deployment and Payment of the Clergy*, had its genesis in these events. It was immediately obvious, from the beginning of my enquiries, that the church was faced with social changes even greater and ecclesiastical structures even more obstructive to its role than Church Assembly realized. Moreover, that the clergy, who never appeared to have been systematically consulted about the church before, were more shrewd observers of the scene than some imagined.

Evidence of social change

The ordinary clergyman does not have to put on theological or even sociological spectacles in order to learn of the changes in society. The abler he is in his pastoral role, the more quickly they strike him, though not necessarily in a spectacular way. A motorway, a new school, a housing estate—these, in Britain, may be the shapes in which the new society appears. Church of England parsons are well equipped collectively to observe changes. Their parishes cover just about every inch of the land. If their parishioners vanish from their customary streets before the bulldozers they themselves cannot simply upsticks and follow (as American churches and ministers are able to do). Their cure is to a territory, and legally to all the souls in it. The most desolate slum clearance area may still have its dusty church and parsonage and lonely clergyman in charge of a parish of broken bricks and stray dogs. Lonely though he may be, he is still a potential outpost of social intelligence.

It was in this spirit that many parish priests responded to my invitation to describe to me the changes in their parish life. What they reported is experienced in some degree by all ministers of religion: it is therefore of universal value to recall what some of them said.

One parish priest spoke of a rural living where little had changed down the centuries until, in the space of a few years, his village was invaded by urban overspill and three new housing estates were built. It is, of course, the sad fact that housing estates seldom produce diversified communities. Much new housing tends to zone people by income-bracket. His new estates were therefore socially as well as physically separated. One was a housing estate, another of semi-detached owner-occupiers, a third was part of a stockbroker belt. With the original village, this gave the parson care of four separate social enclaves as well as the task of bringing all of them into some community relation. (It is an interesting commentary on our society that the church appeared to be the only agency consciously struggling to build a community.) What had to be overcome was the suspicion of each estate for the others and their reluctance to mix—and the failure of the church if it became identified only with *one* income-bracket group.

It is almost an epitome of urban social problems. The village with its ancient corporate life felt overwhelmed by the change, its identity lost. Once a village moves to the status of a town its inner core is usually utterly transformed. The little lanes and paddocks go. The one-way streets and car parks take over. The personal small shops go: the impersonal Woolworths, Marks and Spencers, and the supermarkets move in. The new schools and factories spring up on the outskirts. But the loss of an old community sense does not mean the acquisition of a new one. This has been discovered in towns too, where neighbourly but rundown slum streets have been replaced by bleak tower blocks.

The housing estate

At the other end of the social spectrum are the parish priests who wrote about their housing estates. The village priest faced with new building has at least the *possibility* of a mixed community to serve. The housing estate is normally monochrome. Jobs, interests, speech levels, incomes, standards in home making and T.V. viewing are all much the same. Estate policies and low density building may impose the visual monotony which caused a young witness to the Albemarle Committee to speak of his estate as 'a graveyard with lights'. The professional people and other natural community leaders—teachers, doctors, district nurses, welfare workers, youth leaders—tend to live outside and to come in for working hours only. The brightest sons move out into areas more appropriate to their careers. Besides, estates grow old more or less uniformly. They tend to begin with young couples with throngs of little children. Twenty-five years on the children have moved away. In out-county or out-borough housing estates they cannot retain tenancies of the houses they were born in once their parents have died. The estate therefore has become elderly. It may take two generations to get an age distribution which corresponds with any normal mixed city suburb.

My correspondents revealed other parochial problems. One spoke of his inner town parish as an international transit camp in which no one struck any roots, or wanted to, and where the best of local citizens were ashamed to admit to where they lived; another of his parish of decayed victorian housing as bedsitter land, where anonymity was accepted as the norm and loneliness was the invisible human destroyer.

The social problems reported were not confined to urban areas. One priest spoke of the social destruction of his semi-rural parish by the closing down of its single coal pit, the sole source of employment; another of the transformation brought by the motor car—everyone who could get away on Sundays did; another of how his simple seaside village, with a winter population of 1,000, grew to nearly 10,000 in the summer through caravan and holiday camps—the whole village lived on and for this annual invasion; yet another wrote of how the week-end tripper overspill from the motorway had turned a quiet village into a Sunday 'Elephant and Castle'; yet another spoke of so high a degree of population mobility in his parish that he was lucky if he could depend on keeping a server, a choir-boy, a Sunday School teacher, a sidesman for much over a year.

The motorways

If motorways tended to take the city and its standards as far as the motorway terminus, the new city motor roads created new social problems. As many reported, they destroyed ancient parishes, carved through natural communities and turned places which existed in their own right into mere channels for vehicles —'places to go through'—isolating homes from schools, children from parks, the elderly from the shops, churches from parishioners. Since those reports from correspondents there is evidence of new social problems created by efficient town-planning itself. Where fast motor roads surround one or more neighbourhoods and the neighbourhood group is made self-sufficient with shops and schools and welfare and recreational facilities, a kind of social 'deep-freeze' can occur; an income-bracket ghetto can be created.

To speak of all the changes going on as disastrous would be silly and unjust. Many of them are the result of brave and hopeful attempts not only to house growing populations and to rid ourselves of our inheritance of victorian slums, but to provide new urban environments in which housing and open spaces are linked, the car is segregated from the pedestrian, and genuine communities can come into existence. The point of all this is that the pace of change is so fast that it bears heavily on the lives of all citizens. All their institutions are affected, perhaps the churches most of all, because church structures come down to us relatively unchanged from more stable times. Those ecclesiastical forms and structures were meant to rely on the permanence of the communities in which they were embedded.

Parishes in decay

In my Report I attempted to classify parishes as 'successful', 'decaying', 'other', on the basis of information received from my Main Questionnaire and also to classify parishes by evidential value. This produced the figure of approximately 31 per cent of parishes reporting 'considerable social change'. Moreover, one in four of the parishes reporting this was 'also passing through some form of parochial decay'. Looking at the decaying parishes themselves, I came to the conclusion that social change was the principal cause of parochial decay. 'Eight out of ten parishes classified as decaying were also reporting considerable social change.' I make this point to show that it is possible even statistically to arrive at an estimate of the degree of pressures upon the ancient forms of the Church of England. To understand those pressures in all their frightening enormity it is necessary to look at other aspects of the church's life.

In an institutional sense churches in Britain and Western Europe seem to be static, threatened with decay or actually decaying. Europe is already familiar with empty churches and cathedrals which have become mere museums. At a time of rising population membership rolls and actual congregations decline. Between 1933 and 1965, for instance, the membership of the Methodist connexion in Britain declined from 856,000 to 700,000; and the number of local preachers from 35,000 to 25,000. The Church of England, which baptized 7 out of 10 infants in 1902, baptized only 5 out of 10 in 1962. In 1911 the church confirmed 4 out of 10 persons between 12 and 20; in 1964 only 2½ out of 10. In 1844 almost all marriages—9 out of 10—were Church of England marriages; in 1962 only half—5 out of 10. Church of England electoral rolls which collected 1 person in 18 (152 per 1,000 population over 17) in 1927 had fallen to about half that ratio by 1964 (81 per 1,000). Since 1955 Methodist ordinations fell from 130 to 58 per annum; Church of England ordinations in 1956 were 861, ten years later 667. It would be possible, I think, to show comparable figures of decline for all the major churches of Europe.

It is true that we have, under the encouragement of Dr. Martin (see particularly his *A Sociology of English Religion*), to scrutinize carefully our use of the word 'decline'. Changes in church-going practice, as for instance attendance once on Sundays instead of twice, do not themselves constitute 'decline'. A falling-off altogether in church attendance need not mean a decline in basic religious allegiance—this seems to be true of England, where all institutions are suspect to the working-class and it is firmly believed that 'one does not need to go to church in order to be Christian'. Figures for confirmation or ordination are going to fluctuate with population curves, and church attendances and related figures with population migration. One accepts the necessity for caution: nevertheless, I think that the figures for the century show that there has been a decline, even a serious decline, in what we might call religious institutional loyalties.

Dr. Martin finds the stability of the figures which censuses of all sorts produce about declarations of religious allegiance remarkable and important: I myself in my own Report drew attention to this interesting consistency, which Dr. Martin summarizes as follows: 'Those who identify themselves as Church of England make up two thirds of the English population, or a significantly smaller fraction if Wales and Scotland are included. The Free Church constituency for the whole country stands at round about one person in ten. Roman

Catholic identification reaches roughly the same order of magnitude. The Church of Scotland is of course the majority church in Scotland, but taking Britain as a whole it too has a constituency of somewhat under one person in ten. Thus these four groupings account for the great bulk of denominational difference, leaving only something under one tenth unaccounted for.'

That one tenth has to cover Jews, Eastern Orthodox, Muslims, Hindus and fringe sects. Only about half the tenth—5 per cent of the population—'account themselves as not having any religious label'.

Many parsons of my acquaintance grind their teeth at such bland demographic analyses. Faced with back-breaking chores and empty pews and the fact that only about 1 or 2 per cent of their parishioners (and usually the same lot) attend on Sundays, it does not mean a thing to them that two thirds *say* they are Church of England. One must sympathize. Nothing is more discouraging than supporters who don't support. Yet no sociologist can dismiss such evidence. The reluctance of people to refuse a religious label has deep social significance, and we have to evaluate it against the loaded arguments about secularization we find in such works as Harvey Cox's *The Secular City*. Even if people exaggerate, or wish to exaggerate their attachments in the religious sphere, this exaggeration, as Dr. Martin points out, is in itself significant.

Dr. Martin manages to be reassuring about church attendance too. He thinks it probable that the same total number of people come to church as in the past 'but simply appear less frequently'. Just not going twice on Sundays affects the figures. He goes on, 'the important and massive fact remains that with every incentive to spend time in an alternative manner one quarter of the population is in church at least once a month'.

Of course, this raises the question of 'the great section of the population, which passes by the name of the working classes, lying socially between the lower middle class and the "poor"'. The point is that this class, numerically the greatest, must have declared its religious identification like the others in all those censuses. On the whole, it is the least likely to announce atheism. It must too find itself proportionately represented (though *what* proportion is open to question) in the quarter-population getting to church.

About this class Dr. Martin has many things to say. It 'remains, as a whole, outside of all the religious bodies, whether organized as churches or as missions; and as those of them who do join any church become almost indistinguishable from the class with which they then mix, the change that has really come about is not so much *of* as *out of* the class to which they have belonged...' He roots this working class resistance in the cultural separation of the Anglican Church (in particular) from the masses by 'the chasm of class', in working class resistance to institutions of all kinds and to any major involvement in voluntary associations, including trade unions, and in nineteenth century religious and social alienation. Again, 'the English working class remains one of the most unrevolutionary and one of the most irreligious in the world'. All this is so closely argued, and against French and American experience in particular, that it is almost unfair to pick up sentences, crucial though they are.

Yet some grave questions remain. It is the working class who benefit most from religious instruction in schools—a key figure for Dr. Martin in the ethos of the nation is the lady teacher of divinity in primary schools—and at school assemblies and at football matches and even in pubs joyously sing hymns and who watch 'Songs of Praise'. It is working class children who get to Sunday schools and into the Scouts, and working class boys and girls who like to get married in church, and working class people who adore royalty and who followed intensely every televised element of the coronation. What I am trying to say is that the exposure of the working class to extra-mural religious influences is high, and life-long and effective on the distaff side. This is the only way one can explain that pretty general 67 per cent adherence in England to the Church of England (without working class adherence it would be nearer 7 per cent!): it must to some extent explain the quarter which gets to church. Is Dr. Martin's verdict on the working class ('most irreligious', 'outside all religious bodies' and generally totally alienated) really on all fours with his evidence of the religious ethos of society as a whole? I think there is a dilemma of interpretation here which leads him to have his cake and eat it.

The fall into sclerosis

It used to be said that what appeared to be a bad thing—the fall in membership—could be a good thing in disguise. What the churches were losing were their conformist members, and good riddance to them: those who remained were the hard-core Christians, the faith's bedrock. This is too superficial, as well as too flattering, a view. The churches and sects which are running down are above all those which are failing to recruit young people, or losing them faster than they win them. The hard core tends to be the elderly, for whom church membership has become part of a way of life it is necessary to hold on to the *more* the world drifts away. It is almost central to the contract of elderly membership that the church should change as little as possible. Declining churches tend to be left not only with an elderly membership but also with sclerotic forms. In the same way, declining recruitment to a ministry not only means falling numbers but also an ageing ministry. The all-round results of decline can be therefore to set a church farther and farther away from the centre of the world it is designed to serve.

The relationship between decline and urbanization

My Report, if it did nothing else, showed up one important statistical fact, that the decline in the measurable pastoral results of the Church of England was far from even. The dioceses where results were high, which retained, so to speak, the patterns of 1911, were rural dioceses. The dioceses where results were worst, were the highest density urban dioceses. It mattered little whether it was baptism, confirmation, marriage, average Sunday attendances, Easter communions, recruitment to the ministry—in each, there is a consistent fall in results per 1,000 of the population as one moves across the spectrum from rural dioceses such as Hereford to urban ones such as Southwark, Birmingham, London. The mean confirmation rate 1961–3 per 10,000 population aged 15 and over for Hereford diocese was 109·2; for London diocese 29·5: and this is but a single example. But of course the point is that urbanization is indisputably on the increase. We may expect therefore pastoral results to fall from a rural to an urban level as more and more rural areas become urbanized. It is not too much to say that, from the Church of England's point of view, the great conurbations are becoming mission areas. What often disguises this urban failure is the fact that, given a large parochial population, 10,000 say, one can have quite a reasonable church attendance on Sundays and a lively church life. The church congregationally is a success. But as a Christian mission and a pastoral service it may be touching only a tiny fraction of the population. How insignificant this fraction can be in the worst areas came out in a Battersea Deanery Survey made in 1965–6.[1] Of the population of England 66 per cent are baptized into the Church of England, 24 per cent confirmed, 7 per cent are on electoral rolls, 6 per cent are Easter communicants and perhaps 10 per cent attend church. A count in Battersea deanery of main service attendance at Church of England churches on a given Sunday gave 942 persons out of a population of 110,076 —less than 1 per cent. Even Christmas and Easter communion figures hardly doubled that. There are 16 Church of England churches in the deanery and 14 other places of worship (Roman Catholic and Nonconformist). Attendance at the other places is not known, but it is hardly likely that total attendance at the main Sunday services in this (former) London borough is anywhere near the urban, let alone the national, average. Battersea is, of course, one of those inner town areas, the population of which has fallen through bombing, slum clearance, new low density building and urban renewal generally. It is not a-typical.

If looked at from a rural point of view, the Church of England is holding its own: from an urban point of view it is in retreat and disarray. It seems fantastically ill-equipped and ill-devised to cope with urban problems.

Where the clergy aren't

The situation has to be looked at statistically to show how absurdly the clergy is deployed and how ineffectively in relation to urban needs.

1. 10·5 per cent of the population is grouped in livings of under 2,000 population and has the services of 38·2 per cent of parochial clergy.

2. 55·8 per cent of the population is grouped in livings of between 2,000 and 9,999 population and enjoys the services of 45·2 per cent of the parochial clergy.

3. *33·7 per cent of the population is grouped in livings of*

10,000 population and over and enjoys the services of only 16·6 per cent of the clergy.[2]

In fact, one can take the analysis a stage further, and it is then even more frightening in its implications. There are 99 parochial livings with populations of 20,000 and over. This gives *at least* a population of two and a half million in the care of 99 incumbents (with a curate force of 269 to help them). At the other end of the scale, in parishes under 1,000 population, something like 3,500 clergy look after about three million people.

What emerges from this is that the Church of England is still largely oriented to rural England and only half-heartedly concerns itself with great cities. And this is the consequence of its structure. Its parishes are geographical units primarily; it is ground rather than population they are organized to cover. There are good historical reasons for this, but reasons good enough for past ages are not necessarily satisfactory for this. Down the centuries, the almost inflexible parochial system enforced the rule that a parson had to be sent to a benefice which would (theoretically) 'keep' him. He could not simply be sent to an area of need. He could only serve parochially with another clergyman if one of them was a curate. Even if a parish was a cure of 50,000 souls, two *incumbents* could not serve it together. However inconvenient socially and pastorally, a new parish would have to be carved out of the old to increase the clergy-power even by one man of 'vicar' status. At least this was the situation when I made my report.

The geographical inflexibility has been supported up to now by the legal freehold. A parson could not be moved from his living so long as he fulfilled his statutory duties and committed no crime. Nor, if he wanted to, could he move himself to another living. This did not freeze men; on the whole they moved about fairly fast, and still do.[3] What it did was to prevent the best use of men. As we shall show, the new Pastoral Measure will change many things and *Partners in Ministry* still more, if it is approved, but it is true all the same that when men move at the moment is is not by the common will of the church, and perhaps not even at the guidance of a bishop, but frequently because some quite obscure patron who need never himself go to church or say his prayers has the gift of a living which has fallen vacant or because a church society was smart enough in the last century to buy up livings in order to enforce a particular brand of churchmanship on parishes it 'owns'. It was for such reasons that I spoke of patronage in my Report as follows:[4] 'patronage by private individuals, by colleges, by religious patronage trusts defies any justification except the pragmatic one that men might be found this way and in no other. It is the oddest principle indeed that compels a college to offer livings to its members: and an irrationality which does the Church moral harm if a patronage society or religious trust owns advowsons and uses them to determine parochial appointments of the colour of churchmanship it approves. One can imagine the outcry in the press if it were discovered that a political party "owned" the right to make civil service appointments in order to ensure placing men of the right political colour in key posts! Such a dubious system of empire-making within the church could only have grown up because the church was never properly master of its house.

'Patronage also creates endless legal confusion. A title of patronage belonging to trustees or private owners seems often incorrect and legal justification difficult. Where joint or successive ownership or a "trustee" system operates the difficulties of legal title increase. Many so-called trustees are not legally trustees, but beneficial owners, for no proper trust deeds exist. Deeds of conveyance, I have been assured, are as necessary as deeds of appointment of new trustees: in one diocese ninety-one titles are said to be out of order. Reform cannot be long delayed for the good of the Church's soul.'

Non-church or new structure?

There are critics who, seeing all these problems, press that the church should have a totally different structure. Some argue that a territorial—or parochial—structure is meaningless. It only functions at all in residential areas (they say), and during the day these are inhabited mostly by women and children; but women too go out to work and children go to school. Suburban parishes can empty during the week and fill up only at week-ends. But the motor car has altered the week-end pattern too—a parish can evacuate itself on any fine Sunday. Because social patterns have so changed that even a whole family may spread its life over the whole human zone rather than live it out in one residential neighbourhood, there are those who say that the parochial ministry can only be to the very old or very young: the vital, productive element of the nation is never reached. Ministry therefore should not be horizontal, territorial, but vertical, directed to man in his various social and economic functions. Christian mission should be to industry, to commerce, to universities and schools, hospitals, prisons, ships. There are many elements of exaggeration in such thinking about the residential parish—it is often rather more than the desert it is argued to be, and the family is still the basic social unit in which concern for others operates at the deepest and most religious level. The criticisms hide an imaginative failure to understand the difficulties of organizing Christian mission in most industrial and commercial enterprises. And as many sociologists have pointed out, basically all mission is territorial—a plant works in *this* locality, the men employed live *there*, an industrial missioner can only, like a commercial traveller, cover so much ground. The more time he spends on travelling, the feebler his efficiency, the weaker his roots, the more tenuous his claim to the loyalties of those he calls upon.

At the other end of the scale are those who would 'non-church' the church.[5] For them Christianity resolves itself down to committed persons. These, it is argued, are the only church we need. They can get along in informal groups with no historical lumber in the shape of liturgy, organization, plant. But this seems only a device for the liquidation of the church. No Christians with a sense of history or of responsibility for their inherited institutions or of care for their professional ministries could accept as a practical policy this retreat to the catacombs. It has the very smell of defeat and discouragement about it.

There remains another attack—as to whether institutions can be reformed and updated, to give them new vigour as well as a closer relationship to the emerging forms of our new society. The recommendations which were an integral part of my *The Deployment and Payment of the Clergy* were drafted with this end in view. My proposals were based on preserving all that was good, on a wise use of resources and on open accounting for what we do.

Proposals of the Paul Report

Two important proposals, which received a great deal of publicity, concerned the placing of the parson in his parish. It seemed to me a palpable absurdity that a priest should be placed in his parish and hedged about with all sorts of protective devices as though he were a baron behind his moat. The freehold seems to me still legally silly and psychologically dangerous —ranging the parson over against the world instead of setting him in the midst of it, which is where Christ was, and as though a man could not function as a priest without special favours no layman normally enjoys. Justice, I thought, would be more than done if the freehold were transformed into a leasehold—if tenure of a living were limited instead of absolute. I proposed a tenure of ten years in the first instance, with the possibility of extension for a further five years. This reform would impose upon the church the necessity for a new care for its manpower. I therefore proposed staff consultations of obligation between the bishop and the priest and others concerned when a man had served seven years in a parish.

It also meant the end of the obscure and malfunctioning system of patronage. Instead I asked for the grouping of dioceses into regions, and for regional boards, professionally served and representative of the dioceses, to have the right of presentation to all livings in the region, but without prejudice to a bishop's right of acceptance of a man. I wanted, too, a system whereby the boards reported to Church Assembly, and could be serviced nationally by a central clergy registry. The trend to regionalization in our social and political planning generally would then have its parallel in the growing regionalization of the church. I anticipated that regional boards might be thought of as isolated 'bureaucratically' from the church, and suggested that they might become provinces. Indeed, new provinces, and a national synod as proposed by the Hodson commission in *Synodical Government in the Church of England*, would constitute an encouraging *aggiornamento* of the Church of England.

Regions would have another value. There ought not to be a 'rural' ministry and an 'urban' ministry in the church, but one ministry. The existence of many mainly rural dioceses side by side with many mainly urban dioceses encourages this unfortunate dichotomy. Regionalization which related contiguous urban and rural dioceses in a common manpower policy could end this.

Putting men in teams

I saw the need for new parochial forms to end the anguished isolation which many clergy reported, the better to serve the new society springing up so swiftly, and the more efficiently to use men. I rested proposals here largely on group and team ministries. Over the last two decades there have been many experiments in group and team ministries. A group ministry is the result of a decision of several parishes to come together and to work their parishes as one area. A team ministry is the decision to work a parish with a team of clergymen, one of whom will be the official incumbent and the others, no matter what their charge, legally curates. But these experiments have no durable legal basis, so they can break down. The curates of a team can decide to go off somewhere where their prestige or security is greater; group ministries can break up because one parish priest decides to opt out, or because a priest dies and the patron whose turn it is does not approve of a group ministry, or even because its legal basis is so vague. I linked advocacy of group and team ministries with arguments for 'a major parish'—that is, the amalgamation of several parishes in an area in need of reorganization to create a new parochial unit run by a college of clergy all of incumbent status. These proposals with some modifications have been embodied in the Pastoral Measure now accepted by Church Assembly, and in general meet the case I made. As passed, the measure will give to Bishops and Diocesan Pastoral Committees considerable powers to reorder the church's work in the areas of greatest need. The Bishop with his Pastoral Committee can draw up 'pastoral schemes' for submission to the Church Commissioners which cover one or more parishes. The schemes may unite benefices or provide for pluralities or establish group or team ministries on a legal basis. In the creation of a team ministry the measure gives power to appoint a rector, the technical incumbent, either as a freeholder or for a limited tenure, and a team of clergy each holding the ecclesiastical office of vicar and having the same security during his term of office 'as an incumbent of a benefice'.

The vicar's tenure is not to be affected by a change of rector, and in addition to the role of vicar he may be licensed by his Bishop to special functions in the team. The clergy status in a group ministry will, under the Measure, be different. Each clergyman will retain his incumbent status and his living, but 'shall have authority to perform in the area of every such benefice [in the group] all such offices and services as may be performed by the incumbent of that benefice'.

A pastoral scheme may not only unite parishes into a new benefice or group them together but provide for the dissolving of existing deaneries or archdeaconries and the creation of new ones.

A scheme may be brought into existence upon Order in Council without the assent of any sitting freeholder such as an incumbent. But if a man is dispossessed of his freehold under the scheme provision is made for his compensation.

The rights of Parochial Church Councils are protected under the Measure. Patrons can, but need not necessarily, lose their rights under the Measure. New patronage rights do not have to be conferred. Schemes can bring together parishes of different dioceses and decide to which diocese the new benefice shall belong.

Beyond question, this is a Measure which will facilitate the growth of what I called in my Report 'major parishes' and of specialized ministries within them. It promises, for the first time, ministries flexible and concentrated enough to deal with new towns, areas of urban decay and renewal, housing estates, linear towns and areas of rural depopulation.

Partners in Ministry

In the Spring of 1965 Church Assembly appointed a Commission under the chairmanship of Canon W. Fenton Morley to consider those aspects of my report which had not been submitted to the Pastoral Commission and other bodies. The Commission's Report was published in June 1967, under the title *Partners in Ministry*.[6]

Its principal proposals are intended to bring about a total revision of the terms of employment of the clergy. Following my recommendations the commission asked for the abolition of private and trust patronage and of the parson's freehold and for placing all ministerial appointments in the hands of statutory church commissions.

Two new kinds of bodies were proposed; the first a Central Ministry Commission appointed by and responsible to Church Assembly (or National Synod), and Diocesan Ministry Commissions bearing the same relation to Diocesan Synods. The tasks of the Central Ministry Commission would be to prepare an effective central registry of the clergy, to appoint certain dignitaries (such as, it would be expected, Bishops and Cathedral Deans and Provosts) and to organize a quota system so that 'clergy-power' can ultimately be deployed in dioceses according to the kind of needs I discussed in my own report. This would include the direction of ordinands (in consultation with their sponsoring bishops) in accordance with both training and pastoral needs.

The Diocesan Ministry Commission would appoint to all diocesan posts, except dignitaries, and in terms of its own pastoral oversight. It would be a strong statutory body with the Bishop as chairman and suffragans and archdeacons as members: there would be lay members and representatives of the public—councillors, teachers, trade unionists, perhaps.

Its powers would be real because of the disappearance both of patronage and the freehold. The terms of entry into the ministry and of tenure of posts would be totally altered. Upon ordination, if the Commission's proposals are accepted, a man will be taken on the 'strength' of his diocese, and will be able to remain on it for the whole of his active service if he chooses. If he goes abroad he can still remain on its 'books'. As a clergyman on the strength he will be housed free of rent and receive the stipend appropriate to his post. The stipend will continue irrespective of whether he is occupying a post or not and even when he is unemployed. The distinction between a beneficed and unbeneficed man instantly goes, the youth chaplain or industrial missioner will be a salaried agent of the church in precisely the same way that a parish priest (effectively) is at this moment. This makes possible the placing of staff irrespective of the benefice system. As many men of incumbent status as may be needed can be placed in a parish of missionary possibilities, a great advance.

All appointments would be for a stated term of years, or else be without a stated term but subject to periodical review.

The Commission argued that to meet the new flexibility of appointment it proposes it would be sensible to pool all the

thousands of separate benefice funds and to create one common
stipendiary fund from which all living and active agents could
be paid. It proposes therefore a Central Payments Commission
(the Church Commissioners) which would work with the Central Ministry Commission to allot the funds necessary (subject
to diocesan augmentation) to maintain the 'quota' of clergy
allotted to it.

In one direction the Report goes beyond my proposals—I had
proposed a leasehold instead of a freehold, to be held for a term
of ten years with the possibility of renewal for five more. The
Commission proposes an appointments system of a completely
flexible kind, with only that guarantee of tenure named in the
terms of appointment.

On the patronage side the Report does not go as far as my
proposals. It makes the Diocesan Ministry Commission the sole
appointing body in its diocese for almost all posts. But it is
important that it should be a real body, capable of making independent decisions, and not a make-believe body simply rubber-
stamping decisions of the bishop at his staff meetings. I was
very conscious, when making my own proposals, that tensions
developed between bishops and their clergy. Men felt they were
lost if they got in the bishop's bad books. This tension is an
impediment to good pastoral care. Therefore, without depriving
a bishop of the right to *approve* a man, I proposed Regional
Appointments Boards serviced by a fully professional staff, each
of which would act as the 'patron' for several dioceses. I
thought that this would relieve the bishop personally—most
bishops are overworked—and make possible more objective consideration of each clergyman's career-structure.

Also, I am convinced that some dioceses are too small, or too
rural or too urban, to maintain an effective deployment policy.
They need to co-operate with adjoining dioceses to bring into
existence a proper balance of available posts for young and old,
active and tired men. For instance, I found it alarming that 32·1
per cent of retired clergy retired *before* the age of seventy—that
is before they had reached full pension rate. I deduced that
many older men were seriously tired or ailing. I also reported
that the most hard-pressed industrial dioceses had fewest light
cures for old or sick men. I defined a light cure as a single
church parish of under a 1,000 population. I wrote, 'Birmingham has 4, Liverpool 5, Southwark 7, Manchester 8, Guildford

10, Portsmouth 10, Derby 11 and Wakefield 11; whereas Oxford has 114, Exeter 94, Bath and Wells 90, Norwich 88' (p. 270). But if in the West Midlands one united five dioceses in a Region (Lichfield, Birmingham, Coventry, Worcester, Hereford) the total of such small parishes would be 153! Uniting six London and Home Counties dioceses (p. 202) would make available 288 light cures for the region. These are serious considerations indeed. It makes me hope that eventually the regional idea will come, or that the Central Missionary Commission will set up regional sub-committees.

Conclusion

The reader will recall that in discussing the church's doctrine of itself I spoke of two great spiritual alternatives: on the one side the juridico-political structure typical of the Church of Rome down the centuries and the other the church, which we perhaps do not really anywhere yet possess, run in the spirit of the Palestinian mission.

But these spiritual alternatives are not translatable into organizational terms with any degree of simplicity. It would be plainly naïve to think, for instance, that if the world churches abandoned the juridico-political model they could therefore move sweetly over into non-organizational forms, into the non-church, for instance. One of the simplest forms of church is Dr. Billy Graham's crusade. He draws great crowds and preaches to them, as Jesus did in Palestine. From them he asks organizationally little or nothing. Yet to maintain his crusade a wealthy and hard-working organization is necessary. Any church in the complex world of today has first to organize in order to be heard. It creates structures, employs men and women, trains and maintains its ministers, supervises and (somehow) deploys them, owns property, builds buildings, publishes, runs conferences, perhaps schools and colleges. It becomes part of the social structure, a status group and a pressure group within society, perhaps the dominant element in the culture, or itself a sub-culture with a degree of independence. In this societal sense it becomes with the years not just a structure in the ordinary sense but a palimpsest of structures. We cannot see churches only in their doctrinal and confessional and spiritual senses, but we have to see them in all their complexity as forms in our highly structured society through which men

C

and women earn their livings and pattern their working lives, and fulfil their longings for status and acceptance. The effort to understand the churches in their administrative and workaday sense, and to see the difficulties there, has dominated this chapter and concerns us in the next. It will take us in Chapter 6 to a study of the relationship of institutionalism to Christian belief.

CHAPTER FIVE

THE PROBLEM OF THE SEPARATED MINISTRY

Churchgoing has declined, but public regard for the priest or the minister may have risen. It is an almost irresistible conclusion. The pages of *Punch* at the turn of the century paraded bishops of a blimpish stuffiness, and endless curates of a Wodehousian imbecility, and the occasional pecksniffian free church minister lifting his eyes to heaven. The parson was fair game in the music hall too. In those days there seemed to be something essentially humorous just in being a parson. Now the humour comes if at all not from the curate braying at the garden party but from the cleric caught out in certain professional situations. If the findings of the survey on *Television and Religion* count for anything, public esteem for the zeal and sincerity, and powers for good of priests and ministers is far higher than anything accorded to any politician since Winston Churchill. Ironically, it coincides with a loss of nerve among all ministerial élites, including the Roman Catholic ministry. Charles Davis's resignation from the church and priesthood and Father Herbert McCabe's dismissal from the editorship of *Blackfriars* in 1966 and 1967 are both symptomatic.

The sacred ministry and the lay ministry

I have already indicated some good reasons for malaise. If the church is held to be the instrument of God in the world, then the priesthood has a role that cannot be too sacred or exalted. The priest stands at the centre of a divine drama. *The Dogmatic Constitution of the Church*[1] explains that, 'In virtue of the sacrament of order, they [the priests] are consecrated in the likeness of Christ, high and eternal priest, as genuine priests of the New Testament, for the work of preaching the gospel, tending the faithful and celebrating divine worship. They do share, at their own level of the ministry, the office of Christ, the sole mediator and they proclaim the divine work to all. Their mightiest exercise of their sacred office is at the eucharistic worship or assembly. There, acting in the person of Christ, they make proclamation of his mystery.' However, what meaning can be attached to such statements today if theology generally, and the new theology especially, place the whole of the New Testament under question and form criticism dissects the Gospels and arrives at the Bultmann position that the Gospels are primarily postcrucifixion myths about, and interpretations of, a virtually unknown life? When the status of Christ is diminished, then the ordained ministry is diminished too, as of his generation and authority. Again, if the new theology rejects the whole realm of the transcendent or 'the supernatural', then the church is put under doubt as the continuing body of a heavenly Lord. Today, in a double sense, the ordained ministry is therefore shaken in its role. Of course we know that Roman Catholic theology is not a new theology. By and large it is Thomist still. Nevertheless, all theology since Barth, Bultmann and Tillich is more radical and questioning than ever before, and doctrinal doubts about the church and the ministry strike deeper than ever. The priest sees his vocation challenged most severely from within the faith.

Simultaneously, Christian thinking lays more emphasis than ever upon the role of the laity in the churches. Churches with their backs to the wall rediscover the silent millions the church triumphant ignored. The priesthood of all believers is now really meant, or partly meant. Even the Vatican Two document moves in this direction. True, it maintains the old directives: the duty of the laity is to seek the Kingdom of God in the transaction of worldly business. They must pray and be faithful and bring up their children in Christ and work with their pastors. 'They should be prompt to welcome in a spirit of Christian obedience the decisions the sacred Pastors make as leaders and directors in the Church, for they are the representatives of Christ.' The nostalgic hankering after a well-disciplined lot, subordinate to the priesthood, is obviously there, but, 'On all the laity, then, falls the glorious burden of toiling to bring the divine offer of salvation even more and more into the reach of men of all times and all over the world. They must have every path opened to a whole-hearted personal participation ... in the saving work of the Church.' The document grows lyrical about layfolk as the agents of Christ. It is hard to avoid the conclusion that almost by accident the laity are being awarded the principal mission of the church. Inevitably, the separated role of the priesthood is put under question.

In a symposium[2] issued by the (Church of England) Advisory Council for the Church's Ministry, C. F. D. Moule remarked that 'the New Testament evidence for any ordained ministry, as such, is so meagre as to be almost negligible'. And F. P. Coleman wrote, 'Language has its own problems and limitations: if we say that all members of the priestly body we call the church are priests, we must find some way of differentiating between the Body as a whole and those who exercise a special ministry within it; otherwise realities will be blurred and our understanding of the truth confused. However we solve the language problem, we must acknowledge that all members of the Church *may* properly be described as priests.'

The most encouraging answer to the question posed about the difference between the laity and the priesthood comes from Martin Jarrett-Kerr—'The higher and nobler the conception of a "lay priesthood", the higher and nobler the conception of the man called to be a leader and an interceder of and for the laity.' But is that really so, or is this whistling to keep the clerical spirits up? A rise in the powers of the laity will not automatically push the clergy on to a higher rank, particularly if the lay role is to embody functions once the monopoly of the priesthood—such as, for example, the distribution of the sacraments.

The point, however, is surely made—that the role of priest or minister is the subject of internal church debate everywhere, and that this is an element in the uncertainty the priest or minister registers today and the confusion which attends the church's doctrine of itself, which I have already examined.

Society's support

If the clergyman finds his role *in the church* harder to define today it must be still more difficult for him to define his role in society. When society supported the church and held its functions in high esteem, then a clergyman's confidence in his functions was supported or his doubts overruled by society's confidence. In a time when the church is at the periphery rather than in the centre of society a clergyman's self-criticism is curiously intensified by the spectacle of social indifference. The world seems to be endorsing his own doubts at least to the extent that it regards churchgoing as unnecessary, and therefore has little use for his traditional functions, even those sacramental ones held to be the justification for his separated office.

Of course, it can be argued that his traditional functions are wrongly conceived, that, for example, it is not the duty of the ministry to bring people into the church but to take the church out into the world. As Professor Gordon Davies says in *Worship and Mission*, 'The Church is not a cultic group concerned with building services, but a body of people charged to join in mission; its specific acts of worship are therefore to be understood, as we have argued constantly above, in terms of mission. The eucharist is part of mission and the dismissal is primarily an echo of the missionary command in Matthew 28. Any and every service is most fittingly brought to an end by a dismissal which expresses this outgoing to the world at large. It is therefore not a cosy rounding-off of a cultic act but part of the sending of God's servants in mission' (pp. 140–1). Of course. But what does one do, whether as layman or clergyman, in 'the world at large'? This is the most difficult question to answer, particularly by the priest himself, who is, intentionally, in a way, 'removed' from the soilure of the world by the ordination service.

In *Further Thinking about the Ministry*, Canon R. S. O. Stevens says, 'The tragedy of our present selection and training of men for the ministry is that they appear launched upon the Church with an almost universal conviction that their task is to serve the church, not to serve their fellow men.' Leaving aside the fact that serving the church was, historically, Christian-wise, thought to be *the way* one served one's fellow-men, one sees what he means. One knows that the pattern of deployment in the Church of England (and not only there) is to specific institutional charges. To build up church societies, to bring more people to worship, to care for the faithful, to instruct the young, in general to build up a vigorous parochial life, *and to look after the buildings*, this every parish priest understands, and every ordinand too. But if this parochial charge is argued to be only a base from which to conduct mission, whether lay or ministerial or combined, one can understand why the clergyman most convinced that this is necessary pauses in confusion to ask—yes, but *how*?

The passing of the one educated man

The traditional role of the clergyman has suffered such changes that he does well to pause. There was a time when the minister was the one educated man in his flock, a repository therefore of learning and wisdom. And even in the nineteenth century, when education was more widely spread, he was likely to be one of the few educated men in his parish, as well as, apart from the poor law guardians, the most important social agency. It is unnecessary to enter into an elaborate analysis of what has changed. In technological skills the clergyman may now be the least educated member of his congregation. The clergyman faces a world taken over by experts. He faces it, often, as a helpless amateur. It is an infinitely complicated world in which all of us, in fields for which we were not trained, are amateurs too who find it increasingly difficult to know what is happening. That world tends to get run by expert sitting alongside expert. This is true of social services too. Precisely how and where is the ministerial service to be given to such a world? Where can the Christian impact be effectual? It is perhaps not unexpected if the clergyman is tempted to stay within those fields in which he is a professional—liturgy, worship, prayer, doctrine, pastoral care for his own faithful. The interesting thing is the clergy awareness that they cannot stay there. In the United States the clergy are very active in the fields of counselling and social work. In Britain clinical theology has reached the status of a clergy movement. Industrial missions and other specialized forms of ministry—hospital, prison and university chaplaincies —have a long history. Ministries to coloured immigrants and to youth continue to grow. We have in England a small group of worker-priests. Yet, though the more sensitive clergy are in fact seeking for an extra-parochial role in society, we can sympathize with the unhappiness of those clergy who do not find themselves fitted for roles other than traditional ones. And they are the majority. It is a consolation perhaps that a similar loss of status and of confidence in contemporary society attends the devotees of liberal and humane studies too. They, too, are often intellectually disarmed by the scientific expert.[3]

Yet another sense of malaise must spring from criticisms of the institutional church which call in question the value of an ordained ministry. It is not unknown for critics to argue that there are too many Church of England priests—the number could be cut back, the standards raised, the bulk of mission work could be done by the laity. The non-church movement would presumably dispense with an ordained ministry altogether. All such arguments must increase the clergyman's sense of being undervalued even within his church—of which another aspect has been persistent underpayment of every kind of clergy. The minister's standard of living lags behind that of other professional men, despite important fringe benefits such as free housing.

An old man's job?

Some Church of England clergy statistics reveal dismaying tendencies. *Facts and Figures of the Church of England, 1966,* shows how, in just over a century, the age structure of the ordained ministry has completely changed. From being a young man's job it has become predominantly an old man's job. If recruitment continues to fall the average age will rise still higher. It is also a profession which is losing its graduate status. In 1963, 47·8 per cent of men ordained were graduates, in 1964, 38 per cent, in 1966, approximately 32 per cent. The tide is rapidly moving against the church at a time when graduation is becoming the minimum professional qualification everywhere else. Just as in age structure, the position occupied a century ago is being reversed.[4]

One can argue from such statistics that the Church of England ministry is going to be professionally at a disadvantage in the world at the moment when its tasks are escalating in size and complexity. And what tasks! The total population of the two provinces is going to rise from 44 million in 1963 to 61 million in 2003: density per square mile will therefore rise from 880 to 1,210 persons. Already, since 1911, the number of parishes of 20,000 and over have doubled. Without question, giantism in parishes must gallop ahead in the next forty years. But while the rest of us will grow thicker on the ground, the clergy will grow thinner.

At the end of 1963 the average number of persons per full-time Church of England clergyman was 2,894. Simply to peg the ratio to about 1 parochial clergyman to 2,500 persons involves raising the number of clergy by about 10,000 in the next forty years. To *reduce* the ratio to 1:2,000, roughly the

1901 position, in that time, means doubling the size of the ministry! When I said similar things in the Paul Report some critics thought the whole idea of such calculations unreal, absurd. They missed the point. And the point is that two things stand out clearly from various statistical exercises—the first is that the *number* of active clergy and laity at work in a given parish appears to be in constant ratio to measurable pastoral results such as confirmation, communicants and so on—and surely also to fellowship?—the second, of course, is that pastoral results generally have an inverse ratio to population density. As population density increases, as the ratio of clergy to population decreases, the already marked decline of the Church of England in effective membership and general support will accelerate. This is the primary lesson of contemporary statistical studies. It would seem a matter of prudence, to say the least, to support and strengthen the ordained ministry at this moment in history while the church has still to find its way ahead.

'God's proper man'

Yet still the ultimate questions have to be asked—what sort of ordained ministry? What relation to the laity will it have? I explored, in the Paul report, the sense in which the ordained ministry is a profession. It certainly is this. Priests, as it were, decide who shall be priests. They set the conditions of entry, the terms of training. Priests control priests. As professionals in terms of liturgy, doctrine, theology, they are guardians and transmitters of a specialized knowledge. In this they resemble lawyers and doctors; in that they service an institution rather than serve a craft or skill, they are more like dons or schoolteachers; as professionals finally responsible to a movement much greater than its officers, or its institutions, they are turned outwards, towards the movement, to which they must account, rather than inwards towards the autonomous profession.

Yet the statements quoted from the Vatican Two document on the church reveal that the priesthood claims a great deal more traditionally than simply to officer a movement, like officials of a trade union. Priests are the vehicle of the divine power into the church, into the world. They are raised up and set apart, a holy élite, a concentrated core of a spirituality which spreads from them into the church. Their relation to the church is similar to the church's relation to the world. Even if we accept the diminished *priestly* role of ministers of free churches—we still have to understand them as vehicles of the Word and under divine inspiration, and not mere officers. Luther called the minister 'God's proper man'.

A ministry so conceived—authoritative, indispensable, bearing an indelible stamp—is highly appropriate to the church conceived as a juridico-political something in the world. Then the ordained ministry is the support of the hierarchy and the field of recruitment for it. It is the source and expositor of church law and doctrine: in that sense it *polices* the church, a function well understood in Luther's day, though nonsensical today in pluralist and voluntarist societies. In such a function the defensive and punitive role of an élite protecting an institution overshadows the loving and mediating role of the anti-establishment Founder. The differences from the spirit and practice of the Palestinian mission could hardly be greater. The role of the ordained ministry today will not become clearer until we decide what the proper Christian presence is to be—or ought to be in this century—and what model we choose for the ministry.

CHAPTER SIX

THE INSTITUTIONAL AND THE CHARISMATIC CHURCH

In the course of my researches for *The Deployment and Payment of the Clergy* it was sharply brought home to me that some clergymen were suspicious of all organizations and institutions except their own parish churches. They were not precisely philosophical anarchists, but in their minds they put the life of the spirit on one side and the life of the institutional church on the other. Buildings, funds, committees, organizational procedures and disciplines, these were the heavy, fleshly limbs of the church with which the spirit was at war. They dreamt, like Teilhard de Chardin, of shedding them. The publication of the Paul Report sharpened criticisms of that sort. It seemed impious to some to deal matter-of-factly and statistically (even though sympathetically) with sacred affairs. It left no room for the Holy Spirit.

Very few laity felt this way. Their impatience was with bad organization and unserviceable buildings rather than with church institutions as such. Working continually with the complex institutions of the world, and at home with them, a very strong lay instinct manifested itself to bring the techniques of the secular world to the solution of religious problems. The laity felt acutely the powerlessness of the church even over its own affairs without good organization. Professionally skilful lay persons saw bad or fumbling organization not as an opportunity for the Holy Spirit but simply as waste, lumber, disgrace.

It is impossible to make sense of the church—any church—in its organizational and social roles without a philosophy (a theology) of institutions and institutional forms, or at least an awareness of the social significance of institutionalization. Of course, the very word 'institution' has to English ears of my generation unfortunate associations. In my youth it was used pretty exclusively about places to be stayed away from at all costs; where today we talk of 'homes', 'hospitals', 'centres', 'schools', then we talked of mental institutions, reform institutions, poor law institutions and the like. The sentence of death on a neighbour in my boyhood was the whisper: 'He's been put away in an institution.' It meant that one would never see him again in the land of the living. The institutions had much in common: architecturally they were grim victorian blocks with echoing corridors smelling of cabbage; they looked like prisons or fortresses. Socially, visitors were not encouraged: the communities were enclosed ones. I know that everyone understands by 'The Church as an Institution' something quite different. Yet I wonder whether discussion of this is not coloured by that old uneasy conception of an institution as something forbidding, self-sufficient and turned from the world. There is a sense even in which to the ordinary man in Britain this could be a satisfactory definition of the church. And among intellectuals, to talk about 'institutionalizing' something carries a jolt with it, as though something free and spontaneous is to be made hard, inflexible, unchanging. As we have seen, among Christian intellectuals and radicals the church is often under attack just for *being* an institution: it has almost as pejorative a sound as establishment: no worse fate then than to be an established institution (of the establishment!), which is certainly what the Church of England is.

The Albemarle Report

Yet let me give another picture. I was some years ago a member of a government committee which took a long, hard look at our youth services. It came back with a blue book which argued a series of reforms. The youth services, we said, lack prestige: they are starved of funds; they are without enough well trained leaders, those they have are paid at less than professional rates. Their clubs and buildings are often dismal places providing table tennis and cups of tea in cracked canteen crockery and so forth, and the young turn up their noses at them. We asked for a new look; clubs which had appeal, good décor, comfort, facilities which competed with commercial enterprises: we thought some of them ought to be in the centre of cities where young people congregated. We demanded higher professional standards of qualification, new rates of pay, permanency of engagement, better public relations, a new advisory council and a new pace-making college. Everyone said 'Hurrah!' and the government accepted our report on the day it was published—not so much a record as a miracle. But what in fact

were we asking for? Wasn't it an *institutionalized* youth service?—something properly established, serviced and defended
in society, with a professional leadership, and an assured and
appreciated place? We wanted it to become part of the pattern
of society, instead of remaining neglected and struggling at the
periphery. To become so it had to be seen and identified: the
more it became so, the better it fulfilled its task. It took its place
among the other institutions we are so busy extending now—
schools, universities, colleges of technology. Can we imagine
how *they* would fare if they were not institutionalized?

Here, then, we are up against institutionalizing as an important process in (contemporary) society. The new idea, system,
culture pattern, whatever it may be, struggles to institutionalize
itself or it risks impermanence or destruction by other forces or
influences: the ultimate in institutionalization is establishment
by law. Of course, the new culture pattern does not function in
an institutional vacuum. Other institutions are there before it,
and it is for a place among them the new 'thing' must fight. Yet
some newly discovered culture patterns fail to institutionalize
themselves formally: their dearest supporters cannot conceive
how to do it. In Europe youth-hostelling long ago moved into
the realm of state institutions, but vegetarianism stays a private
crankiness. Belief or faith easily institutionalizes itself because it
can create a focal image; but how does non-belief, even anti-
faith, institutionalize itself? It is difficult to institutionalize a
negative, a rejection. What is the institution to be identified
with? The Soviet Union, officially anti-Christian, has never
found a way of institutionalizing its offical anti-religiousness.[1]
The religious institutions remain: the new culture-pattern fails
to find its social form. So we recognize that what gets institutionalized is that which lends itself to institution-form. As we
have learnt in England, religion has the institutions; the culture-
pattern is non-religious, and expresses itself not in new institutions but the neglect of the old: they simply become culturally
irrelevant; they may remain institutionally strong if adequately
serviced and financed and seek to justify themselves as cultural
enclaves within a larger, hostile, cultural territory. But this only
disguises their general irrelevance. This is to anticipate discussion of the difficulties of the (or a) church as an institution
in a society which neglects it: there are still gaps in our understanding of what an institution is.

Sociological definitions

The sociological definitions are not as useful as they might be.

Frederick Shippey, in a contribution to *Institutionalism and Church Unity*, gives four American definitions of an institution: '(*a*) as a complex of norms which regulate human activity; (*b*) as a unit of social organization; (*c*) as a system or complex of roles; and finally (*d*) as an eclectic combination of diverse referents into a single configuration or system' (pp. 60–1). Attributes in, or of, the institution are often argued to be 'ideation, structure, purpose, relative permanence, authority, social control, and a specialized personnel'. Typical institutions would be family, school, university, parliament, ministry, church, bank, factory. So that in one sense we can speak of an institution as something naturally given (family), in another (factory) as a form of economic activity, another (school) as a social provision, yet another (parliament) as a form of politico-social control, finally (church) as divinely given. What is common to them all is: (*a*) a powerful regulation of them according to ideas of what they should do, and what for; (*b*) a strong behavioural pattern; (*c*) relative permanence; (*d*) their importance as referents in understanding society; (*e*) a certain visibility and enshrinement of concepts, objectively, about man and his society.

In a 1965 World Council of Churches consultation of the Faith and Order Department on 'Spirit, Order, Organization' we spent much time discussing and defining organizations and institutions in search of a meaning for the ecclesiastical term 'Order'. The definition of the term 'institution' accepted by the consultation, on the suggestion of the sociologists, was 'a pattern of collective behaviour'. By the term 'institutionalization' we came to understand all those processes by which patterns of collective behaviour are established. These may range from spontaneous action at the one end to highly formalized action such as bureaucratization at the other. Any of these processes may lead to rigidity at any stage, but need not necessarily do so.

I demurred with the first definition on the grounds that it could include the trivial and might be challenged on semantic grounds.[2]

What people seem to mean by an institution is something

which has moved from behaviour to a structure which canalizes behaviour: behaviour is not only formalized but organized and self-perpetuating. But I recognize the difficulty that sociologically we have no satisfactory definition of 'institution'. But though definition is difficult, we recognize in the developed 'institution' a strong behavioural pattern, self-perpetuating organization, enshrinement of some doctrine or idea about man.

Everything begins in the heart or mind

I would link institutions with that process which the historian Wilhelm Dilthey described so powerfully—the process of objectification, a process not unrelated to the coming into existence of a common world between men which was the core of Martin Buber's philosophy. Everything, as it were, begins in the heart and mind of man: all the intuitions, insights, visions, intellectual discoveries begin there; but all is eventually lost, even to the individual, if it never escapes from there. To be given value, permanence, identity it has to be communalized and fixed in the cultural milieu. An analogy is useful: the negative in the camera may be the most perfect exposure (or revelation): no one can possibly know it until it is developed, fixed and the prints communicated. So that man takes out of himself the insights of his interior world and objectifies them—by sign, symbol, word, picture, creed, tool, memorial, building, law, social form, political structure, newspaper and so on, endlessly. I would argue that this is basically the process of institutionalization and that it is a key part of the process of culture-creation, civilization-building. Let me give an example—the American constitution is the complete codification—i.e. objectification—of the political ideas of the American revolution expressed in the Declaration of Independence: its whole intention is to give cultural permanency to these ideas and ideals: the Supreme Court constitutes a sacred college to guard and interpret the objectified law. It is a perfect example of the value of institutionalizing.

I have said that churches, religions, have an inevitable tendency to institutionalize. This is because they have a double role—they represent not just an objectification of man's religious experience but a concretization of the divine. They are not only the means by which God speaks to man but they also provide earthly homes for beings from 'another sphere', and the sacred places where special ceremonies show forth or by sacrament communicate the God. This double role gives the religious *buildings* a double value—as witness of a supreme human experience as well as of a supreme godly power. Not only religious buildings but also certain religious artefacts where the religion is still a cultural fact have this special numinous quality, and for this reason communicate a whole culture in a succinct and unmistakable way. One thinks of a Buddhist temple, the Athenian acropolis, a Mohammedan mosque, a Gothic cathedral, a Quaker meeting house, a Jewish scroll, a Communion chalice.

Therefore one has to say, not that churches, religions, ought to institutionalize themselves, but that they have no option! It is part of their witness as well as their function. But that is not all there is to be said, because only at certain golden moments in history is there harmony between the religious institution and the religious impulse it bodies forth and serves, and the society in which it is placed. The height of medieval Christendom might be one such moment when the institutions seemed to have sacralized the whole of a devout and religious society. For the rest the growing religion cannot institutionalize fast enough and chafes because it feels held back: the religion in decline is burdened by the weight of its own history.

The forms of cultic proclamation

Over-institutionalization has another aspect. It is not only that there are too many, too overstaffed, ecclesiastical forms. The same process which makes them supernumerary makes them outdated too. We not only have too many churches in England but those we have are the wrong kind for the present size of our congregations and their liturgical needs. For instance, a contemporary theology which more and more celebrates the role of the laity is set back by building patterns which sharply separate the lay end of the church from the holy end. There the institution in its architectural form is a drag upon the church; it represents the church's spiritual inertia. And it is this sort of evidence which gives force to those who say that to institutionalize a religion is to freeze it, to kill it. They are quite wrong, but we see what they mean, though perhaps we only see it because the cultural pattern is changing. Even the 'freezing' of an institution has its point. If we accept what Gibson Winter says about the church in one of its three forms, the form of 'cultic proclamation' (in *The New Creation as Metropolis*), we can see why it seeks a visible and unchanging liturgical and architectural form. The cultic form (as against the confessional and prophetic forms) declares or sets forth the unchanging eternal in the midst of worldly change and uncertainty. As Gibson Winter writes, 'the cultic church proclaims the Good News through actions or rituals by which the whole of life is conformed with its suprahistorical goal. Men, women and children are incorporated into this mystical life which intersects vertically with the world as a miraculous spiritual body ... The church is, thus, that miraculous organism which mediates eternal life to the members. Salvation and cultic participation become inseparable.' And we might add equally inseparable then is the institutional form. In building, it sharply necessitates just that separation of the holy, miraculous end of the building from the lay (worldly, corrupt) end! There is to be one point only at which vertical and horizontal intersect—and that, of course, is the altar when the priest is there. So that it has to be emphasized that the strenuous effort men make to embody a church in unchanging forms and institutions (including buildings and furniture) has the deepest possible religious significance. It is a mere superficiality if not superfluity to say that a thing has to change, because society is changing, when what it is seeking to represent is non-change, endurance, the eternal. The most that one can say is that the forms by which the idea of the eternal is communicated to one age may be meaningless to another. In any case, one treads warily, reflectively.

Yet as Gibson Winter points out, the church has its confessional and prophetic forms too. In the confessional form it is the *Word* which is unchanging, not so much the institution; in the prophetic form the church is the leaven in the lump of society, the pacemaker of changes from which it could hardly expect itself to be spared. (This is one theme of Harvey Cox in *The Secular City*.) The form of the church affects the form of the ministry. The cultic church is best served by an anonymous holy priesthood, translucent to the godly light; the confessional form by a ministry whose gifts of personality and learning convince in the pulpit; the prophetic form by a lay ministry which dissolves into the world and seeks meaning for the church there. These and similar considerations must lead us to conclude that the relation between the divinely mandated church and its necessary institutions is an extremely complex one which does not easily yield to theoretical treatment, or at least to theoretical simplification.

The ageing of institutions

There is another theme which we must not neglect. It concerns the sheer ageing of institutions. When these are buildings we know that some age into beauty, others into squalor: the one we can accept, the other we deplore. We have no such simple criterion of discrimination when we are faced with the complexity of law, economic and social resources, human officialdom, simple pieties and loyalties which tangle with policies and doctrines to make the ecclesiastical institutions we all know. Institutions are conditioned by their birth. This is certainly so of Christian institutions, in which the Roman Imperial pattern is to be traced. Structure is hierarchical, power flows from the higher to the lower, not the other way round. There is a supreme power; there are the intermediate grades which exercise authority in the name of the supreme power; there is the great mass which is expected to submit, to accept or to be held impious and rebellious. Sharing power with it is not to be dreamt of, because that would mean sharing authority over doctrine. This imperial theory, applied ecclesiastically, has given our church institutions a shape hard to escape. Part of it is the subordination of the laity. And the process of excluding the laity from any role in the church except acceptance is of such long standing, is so built into structures and institutions that we hardly recognize that it is there.

I know it can be said that the Reformation produced a new sense of the responsibility of the congregation for the conduct of the church and the choice of the minister. In Britain we see this at its best in the Church of Scotland and the Congregational Church, where the vestry is still important; but the congregational form soon hardened. The *choice* of minister might remain; the *making* of ministers was reserved. The mediating élite remained in power: the ministry in the upshot was not laicized —the top crust of the laity was clericalized—they became the non-commissioned officers. So that in all the changes of the centuries structure has continued to reflect an idea apparently inexpugnable that a hierarchical institution is alone appropriate to mediate the grace or power which comes through the church from its heavenly founder. *But this does not make very good sense of the doctrine of the priesthood of all believers.* Here we see the weight of a historical form imposing itself: no one can see how it is possible to have a church without an élite unless it ceases to be an institution. But in an age of democracy the church has not come to terms with the idea of an elected élite, and does not know how to.

An example comes from the history of the Church of England: in that long history the only consultative and deliberating bodies of the church were, until 1919, the Convocations of Canterbury and York which hardly ever met together and often did not meet at all separately. The effective organs of government, therefore, after Parliament, were the bishops. As Professor Eberhard Wedell has pointed out,[3] even Convocations after the 1919 reforms failed to be very representative of the inferior clergy in an elective sense: (Canterbury had 89 *ex officio* to 142 elected; York 40 *ex officio* to 71 elected). And, of course, the laity were excluded from Convocations altogether. It was not until 1919 that the work of the Life and Liberty movement led by William Temple succeeded in establishing a Church Assembly in which there was a House of Laity. Even if that House was argued to be representative of the laity (even *clericalized* laity), it is still in Church Assembly a minority group, outnumbered, and subject to veto of other houses, Clergy and Bishops. The reform left the Church of England with three governmental bodies: the two Convocations, York and Canterbury, and Church Assembly. The move to unite the sacred and secular governments in one national synod, including laity, has met with much obstruction. For instance, the lower house of York Convocation said, 'We cannot think it right that there should be taken from the ordained officers of the church the power of final veto. We desire to see the final authority of the church in doctrinal matters vested in the Convocations of Canterbury and York as at present constituted' (i.e. only of clergy). Let it be said that even the existing Church Assembly system of representation really gives only a *token* representation to the laity: as Professor Wedell has pointed out, '15,000 clergy who have roughly the same numerical representation as 2,500,000 lay people.' Even a reformed, single synod would leave the Church of England as a clergy-dominated church.[4] Of course, this can be argued as doctrinally necessary, and this is another matter. *What it is important to see is yet another aspect of religious systems: in addition to their cultural and sacred character they are political systems: they are the instruments, the organizations, by which power is exercised.*

It is important that they should be seen to be such, otherwise we get ourselves into hypocritical contortions of posture, pretending that we are just being pious and holy when we are in fact exercising, institutionally, power over other people. My own report to my church, which was an organizational report, frankly argued for good organization, rationalized institutions as part of the practice of stewardship. Institutional stewardship is as necessary as stewardship over money: in fact, it can hardly be separated from it. It also spoke frankly in favour of the proper maintenance and pastoral care of the ordained ministry and urged policies which would make this possible. Yet, without any particular theoretical intention of doing so, it raised the dangerous question of the role of the clergy as the guardian élite of the institutional church. Whatever else the clergy is, it is also this. Every aspect of institutionalization in society witnesses to the coming into existence of an élite to defend, maintain and exploit an institution—politicians in parliaments and congresses, professors in universities, lawyers in courts, officials in trade unions and so on. The prestige and status of the élite become bound up with the forms of the institution. Anything thought to threaten the élite, even a shift in the balance of power within the institution, is felt as a threat to the institution itself, and vice versa. The élite tends to be conservative in the face of all changes which do not directly increase its own power and status. Hence, on the publication of my report, many clergymen reacted so violently against the threat it contained to the parson's freehold as to identify that freehold with the church. There could be no Church of England without it, they thought. With them, at least, an objective consideration of the church's mission was not possible; their emotional identification with the existing institution was too great: subconsciously it was all a power problem.

Identification of the historic church with the existing institutional pattern is nowhere more obvious than in the legacy of buildings in the possession of all churches in the West. It is quite clear that many of us are 'over-churched'. What do we do with a legacy conceivably culturally valuable as well as sacred?

One society said to me that there were 10,000 English churches which ought to be preserved as of historic value: more than half—since we have nearly 18,000 parochial churches in 11,438 livings. An expanding church would regard these only with joy as instruments of evangelization. The church contracting hardly knows what to do with them: and 'contracting' (although a position from which one can subsequently expand) may be totally inadequate as a description of the changing as well as shrinking relation of the church to the devouring new patterns of secular society where so much is adrift. The church does not want to mortgage the future. On the other hand, it does not want to turn its trained priesthood into caretakers of premises, odd-job men in charge of boilers, graveyards, church roofs. It does not want to produce an ecclesiastical system without laity of which H. Kraemer spoke and which is the danger in the West today.

The opposition between the institutional and the charismatic

There is a clear sense, too (only it is non-sense), running through all church history that the charismatic church and the institutional church are opposed: the one is the enemy of the other. Establish precedents, impose forms, create a juridical structure within the church and the Holy Spirit (it is said) is being dictated to. If he does not function along the church-given norms, then there is no place for him. For these reasons charismatic movements seek to escape from institutions and disciplines into freedom: the first monks in the desert, the vagabondage of the Franciscans, the bareness and quietness of Quaker life: these were conceived in terms of that emptiness, that surrender of human will in which the Holy Spirit finds room and is invited to act: in the institutionalized church (it is said) *man* had already made the decisions. Of course, some results of the purely charismatic church were unwelcome: anarchy and prophetism, for instance, constantly threatened the stability of the newly separated congregation: what new form or demand might not be made tomorrow? how could the first insights be preserved, not lost? On the other hand, institutionalized churches themselves gave birth to charismatic movements —missions, monasteries, pilgrimages, Lourdes, Parish and People, Billy Graham and so on—and spontaneously too, not just as 'policy'—religious bread and circuses. By the same token the charismatic movements, the stronger their initial force, the sooner faced the demand for a stabilization of their forms, a preservation of their insights and a restriction upon new adventures—in other words, they institutionalized themselves.

History does not guide us except to say that without institutions bent on shaping and preserving insights or revelations, these would be lost to us.

We may conclude that there is a crisis for the institutional church everywhere which is not solved by liquidating the institutions nor simply by perpetuating them. What *can* we say? Just that institutions are necessary and leave it to the organic processes of time to solve what should survive, what die? Alas, our modern world does not permit that: day in, day out, it is destroying whole regions, rebuilding, making new. Chances lost may never recur. The institutional problem is only soluble if the church accepts that it is also prophetic, and therefore a source of change within and without. Practically, this involves building in to the churches a critical apparatus, a sociological eye. Only by statistical and sociological analyses can the movements of attitude and opinion, the demographic changes and social upheavals be traced, mapped, analysed. The church can hardly neglect so important and effective an instrument which enables it both to measure what it is doing and not-doing and to foresee in part what it has to do. The sociological eye is the pilot in the ship telling us how to go, and whether and when we ought to tranship. But, also like the pilot, it does not decide the destination. It is one means of helping us to live with our institutions under God rather than simply for them. The criterion here would simply be that the role of the church *is* mission, not maintenance, and the value of an institution ought to be determined by the degree it serves mission, not by the impressiveness or historicity of the institution *qua* institution. Fundamental to the sociological argument is the conduct of sociological enquiries on an ecumenical basis.

The final, if somewhat flat, word has to be that institutions are necessary manifestations of the church, and in that sense they are something more than mere instruments. All in all, they incarnate the church. But they are not finally and irreducibly the church: the forms can, and must, change as the objective historical situation dictates. If they do not change, they fossilize, they ossify. The dead coral holds down the living. However, all churches feel the danger of ossification today. As ecumenical pressures grow and reunion appears at last possible, the problem everywhere is how to cast off institutional forms which are barriers to reunion. Perhaps because we are conscious of this, the other side of institutionalization, the side of necessity, is not so easy to understand. But it is there, and in the very beginning. The church was founded on a simple sacramental and memorial meal: in the command, 'Do this in remembrance of me', Jesus institutionalized the relationship between himself and his followers for all time. To speak of 'The Body of Christ' is unconsciously to bear witness to that. Almost everything has been built (and sometimes over-built) around the divine command. Our need is to preserve that sacred fellowship, that divine vocation, in a world rolling over on itself in the fever of social and economic change. For in it we find the source of charisma, the channel of the flow of divine love into the world.

CHAPTER SEVEN

THE GOD-SHAPED BLANK

The *Oxford English Dictionary* defines transcendence as the action or fact of transcending, surmounting, a rising above [something else] and specifically, of the Deity, 'the attribute of being above and independent of the universe'—as distinguished from immanence. There is also another definition, from literature, of transcendence as exaggeration, hyperbole, taking off into the stratosphere, which we might seize on ironically in the present state of affairs.

The second definition, concerning the Deity, seems to me historically the Christian position about God, as it is historically the position of Judaism, Christianity's nurse and begetter. Indeed, in the thought of both, God is so far above and independent of the universe that he was present before it and according to the Genesis myth called it into existence out of nothing. Transcendence could hardly be more completely expressed, since the created world becomes by this doctrine utterly contingent upon the Divine predecessor. The doctrine is spelt out in themes of Divine judgment on the world, the redemption of the world by God and eschatological themes of an ultimate God-given end to all things. It is impossible to consider these themes as merely archaic and passé when a thinker of the calibre of Teilhard de Chardin re-establishes them within a framework of evolutionary philosophy. He sees the whole evolutionary process as an ascension to God at the Omega point—'the end of the world'. The ascension would be pointless were not God above and beyond his universe and calling it to him.

Transcendence as an explanation

The transcendence of God is the most powerful element in *the explanation* Christianity proffers for the understanding of Jesus of Nazareth. His origin is divine. He is the Son of God. He is *sent*. It is intended that he should become man. The fact that his adoption of humanity, his presence among men, reduces the 'distance' between man and God only emphasizes the fact (for our present purpose) of *distance*. A totally immanent God would not be in need of such an intervention. Indeed, in a way, the aboriginal 'distance' is restored by the Ascension, for where Jesus is going his disciples cannot follow. The doctrine of the Holy Spirit, completing the trinitarian conception of God, partially compensates for the absence of Jesus. For by it we are not only intended to see God as 'above and independent' but also 'involved' in his universe. One is entitled, of course, to say that all this is myth, or mythological language. But that does not help us very much, for it is what the myth is telling us which is important. If we take *that* seriously we cannot avoid the conclusion that Christianity has always conceived of God as 'separate' from his creation, able if you like to control his 'distance' from it, or 'involvement' in it, in fact inescapably 'transcendent'. I would go further and say that the doctrine 'God the Father, God the Son, and God the Holy Ghost' is not just a pretty way of saying things, but expresses a metaphysical concept—this is how the universe is constructed, this is how it works, this is the final reality man must reckon with.

Christian dualism

Indeed, coming down the centuries, and looking at Christianity socially and historically, one can only be struck by its dualism: I am speaking about an ontological dualism of the cosmos, not Cartesian dualism, though that is present too in doctrines of soul and body. It is necessary to the doctrine of revelation itself. It is present in St. Augustine's contrast between the cities of man and the city of God; in his predestinationism; in the Reformation controversy over faith and works; in perennial doctrines of grace as that which is not to be commanded but comes to man 'from the outside'. Indeed, it is arguably present in the great social movements of the West, in communism and pacifism, for example[1]—the world is not acceptable just as it is, there are other standards by which it is to be judged, there is a more perfect way of life to which by work and pain and sacrifice man can be brought. Here, in such movements, which spring perennially from Christian soil, we have pure examples of the secularization of Christian dualism. If it were possible to summarize the Christian doctrine in a phrase it might be—the refusal to accept the world as it is, or at all. But that refusal stems from—is only possible *because* of—the conviction of the existence of a Divine Other, and of a Divine alternative for this world. The whole thing swings round and round the concept of transcendence, and it is this concept which has taken the hardest of knocks from the new theology and about which therefore there is the greatest of confusion.

Ronald Gregor Smith (in *The New Man*) said 'the old doctrine of transcendence is nothing more than an assertion of an outmoded view of the world'. Paul van Buren has said that modern man has difficulty in understanding any words which refer to the transcendent. John Robinson (in *Honest to God*) is strongly hostile to all words which refer to God as 'out there' or 'up there'—in fact, to any spatial analyses or metaphors (except 'depth') which might be held to imply that separation or distance I have spoken of as traditional Christian doctrine, and on the grounds that they imply an inacceptable concept of substances (divine and human) or an unverifiable metaphysical system. He writes, interestingly, in a commentary on Tillich's choice of 'depth' rather than 'height' as the preferred substantive about God:

'The Epicurean gods, serene in their empyrean above the cares and distractions of this world, are the epitome of "sublime" indifference. And Browning's supreme affirmation of optimism, "God's in his heaven: all's right with the world", strikes the modern man somewhat more cynically. For if God is "above it all" he cannot really be involved.

'Yet we are not here dealing simply with a change of symbolism, important as that may be. This is not just the old system, in reverse, with a God "down under" for a God "up there". When Tillich speaks of God in "depth", he is not speaking of another Being *at all*. He is speaking of "the infinite and inexhaustible depth and ground of all being", of our ultimate concern, of what we take seriously without reservation ... the deepest springs of our social and historical existence.'[2] And he goes on to quote Tillich again to the effect that 'the name of this infinite and inexhaustible ground of history is *God*'. 'Perhaps you should call this depth *hope*, simply *hope*.'

It is Tillich too who has written that one must not establish a 'super-world' of divine objects. 'You must forget everything traditional that you have learned about God, perhaps even that word itself.' And again, 'the protest of atheism against such a highest person is correct'.

'In our time, in our history, in our existence'

Thomas J. Altizer, in *Mircea Eliade and the Dialectic of the Sacred*, has said that 'the first requirement ... is a forthright confession of the death of the God of Christendom ... Furthermore, we must recognize that the death of God is a historical event: God has died in *our* time, in *our* history, in *our* existence'. Of course, he has said more than is implied in the quotation, and to this we shall refer. But he has said what is in the quotation: and Ronald Gregor Smith has spelt out the meaning of all this in *Secular Christianity*, explaining (pp. 158 f.) the emergence at the end of the European middle ages of the Renaissance man and of a (secular) view of man's life which in the end 'threw off the bonds of a specific metaphysic' as the final truth about man. 'This metaphysic allowed room for a doctrine of revelation and of grace which taught that man's life was completed by the super-imposition of divine powers upon his natural existence. There was thus presupposed a cleavage between the natural and supernatural sphere, and between the sacred and profane.

'With the rejection of this metaphysic there went a slow but steady rejection, covering in turn every activity of man's spirit, of the realities which this metaphysic attempted to represent. Today we have reached the point at which the straightforward secularist finds the "God-hypothesis" simply irrelevant. But more, with the relinquishment of any need to hold on to a realm of "supernature", there has also gone the loss of any felt sense of transcendence.' He defines the death of God in two ways—the rejection of a specific metaphysic and the idea of God it sustained—then the dropping out of God himself and His replacement by 'a God-shaped blank'. This is the condition in secular life and in his own life, with which modern Christian man has to reckon, Robinson, Smith, van Buren, all agree. It could be summarized as the total meaninglessness in modern conditions of traditional Christian language. Paul van Buren has added to this post Renaissance thinking all that comes out when logical positivism and linguistic analysis look at religious language and thought and has argued that Christianity can be completely secularized, the element of the divine and the transcendent completely removed and Jesus followed and revered as the man, the exemplar, of perfect freedom and that this is all that we can mean when we speak of him as God. This is among the most relentless and honest of contemporary reductions of Christianity to secular terms. Harvey Cox, in *The Secular City*, speaks of this drive over into complete secularism as the *intention* of Christianity and of Judaism before it. Both these religions exhibit, he argues, a steady historical purpose to free man from superstitious dependence on the animistic gods of groves and hills and the metaphysical gods of cities and to compel man to utter self-reliance, to that maturity or coming-of-age of which Bonhoeffer spoke. Man is to be forced by God to live in the world as though God is not. This is the ultimate paradox of Christian secularization.

The appeal of the new theology

I, like many Christians today, see the force and appeal of much that is being said, for Christianity is passing through a crisis of belief: through a theological not simply a social crisis, it has been said: it carries not simply less and less conviction into the world but less and less *meaning*. We should all hope to see both meaning and communication restored and sense brought to the human (secular) condition, even if we are not Christians. There is something undignified in a great world system, a *weltanschauung* petering out in 'a general mess of imprecision'—'not with a bang but a whimper'. Yet however much sense there is in the secularizing movement in theology as a left-wing critique, rubbing Christianity's nose in the dirt, reminding us of our concern with this world, if it took over, if it became total, as shall we say Aquinas was once total, then we should witness several abandonments—God would be dismissed as Father (separate in being: creator, corrector in function); Jesus as Second Person, as Son of God; the Holy Spirit as the movement of God from outside the universe or the person to the inside—in fact, the whole realm of the transcendent as once understood. The meaning of Jesus would have to be sought, as van Buren seeks it, in a purely human context and the old theological terms (God, Spirit) given a human and secular evaluation, rather as Tillich at moments intends, though rather obliquely. The meaning of God, the significance of the divine would have to be extrapolated from certain human conditions and activities: man would reveal God, not God reveal himself to man.

Whether this would be successful or not as a reshaped, non-religious faith (in Bonhoeffer's sense) is questionable. Van Buren says of it—

'One wonders where the left-wing existentialist theologians have found their "modern man". A man who shares the empirical spirit of the age cannot interchange these statements about God and man at all. For him, oblique language about God is no more useful than "objectifying" language about God. The problem lies in the word "God" itself, and in any other word supposedly referring to the "transcendent" ' (p. 68).

And if this reduction proved successful, Christianity would have to find its total meaning, total satisfaction as a faith in a 'this-world' context. It would be saying 'there is nothing coming into the world from the outside' or 'man has no resources beyond himself': it would also have to say that early Christianity—or even Christianity down to this century—was mistaken in the conclusions it drew from the Old Testament and from the life and passion of Jesus, and that Jesus was mistaken in his appeals to the Father. It is doubtful whether any world-religion could survive such self-conviction of error. But if it did survive, what would it survive *as*?

Judgment on the world?

The whole world importance of Christianity is that it pronounces judgment on the world and from a source standing outside the world, and not to be commanded or corrupted by the world. It judges the world's evil and describes much of it as sin, and sin as disobedience to God. Jesus himself is shown as suffering the extremity of the world's evil as a voluntary undertaking to reconcile God and man. And all that follows, the establishment of—or the longing for—Christ's kingdom on earth is the contrasting of a Godly way of life with a fallen way of life. I am not at the moment casting judgment on this dualistic conception of the universe: I am simply saying that right or wrong this is what, on its own record, Christianity has always been. Moreover, I believe it is this which has made it the shaker of the foundations of the world, a world religion more dynamic than others. With shattering self-confidence, it presented an Absolute to the world.

If now it becomes monistic, not dualistic, and moreover, monistic in an empirical, pragmatic way, rejecting, like contemporary philosophy, all metaphysics, not simply Christian metaphysics, it must accept the world roughly as given, without expecting an explanation of its source or destiny beyond anything that science or evolutionary theory can give, and without pretending to a natural theology or any theory of creation. If it does strive to judge the world or change it, it will have to do so by the authority of what appears to it the best in human circumstances themselves—with Christ as the finest man. But the best will be the human judgment of human agents, once the transcendental claim has gone. Bonhoeffer's still godly Christ, the man for others, becomes inevitably therefore the man of freedom of van Buren—revered and awesome in his integrity, but with no more authority than his own manhood or genius, with no dimension from himself into the realm of the Divine Other. Here would be the material still for a humane secular faith, but it would be the mere shadow of Christianity's former stature as the earthly channel of a divine, external power. It would become what some sociologists (Bryan Wilson, for example) argue it already is—a kind of social relic.

Refurbishing transcendence

It is not therefore surprising that not all the new theologians go all the way with Paul van Buren, but seek instead for another interpretation of transcendence, for a transcendence which in fact goes some way towards the justification of Christianity as the historic world-changing faith I have argued it to be. There is, to begin with, an obvious ambiguity about the concept of 'depth' which John Robinson picks up from Tillich and exploits so eloquently: 'depth' readmits the mystery and loneliness of God. Tillich wrote, in *Shaking of the Foundations* (and Robinson quotes): ' "Deep" in its spiritual use has two meanings: it means either the opposite of "shallow", or the opposite of "high". Truth is deep and not shallow; suffering is depth and not height. Both the light of truth and the darkness of suffering are deep. There is a depth in God, and there is a depth out of which the psalmist cries to God.' And in another place he speaks of 'depth' as the same thing as the infinite and inexhaustible ground of history, and of God, not as Supreme Being, but as the infinite and inexhaustible depth and ground of all being. Surely there is a restatement of 'distance' here between man and God? The depth of my own spirit or being is that which it is most difficult to plumb: one never senses that one's being is exhausted by the most profound inward look. Hume spoke of the impossibility of finding the self—Bertrand Russell of the discontinuous person. Is there a depth beyond that plumbed by me? (If not, however can I become, as Tillich says, 'estranged from the ground of our being'?) A depth which can be estranged is Tillich's God. But here, surely, is transcendence *upwards*, if I may use the expression which comes from the French philosopher Jean Wahl. The God of depth is ultimately as 'beyond' me as the God of height and his separate ontological being is not really explained or accounted for—or removed—by a change of spatial metaphors.

The same problem arises from the use of the word 'ground'. For 'ground' is ambiguous. If we mean by it that out of which a plant or a tree grows, then it is ontologically distinct from the plant, and a 'distance' is created which is all the same (to me) as transcendence (in height). If we mean what ground means in 'ground floor' perhaps we have a sense in which God as ground is not ontologically distinct from man, in which case we hardly know what it means to invoke him, let alone to worship him.

The lay theologian John Wren-Lewis has gone further than most in refuting 'distance', 'separation', 'transcendence' in God. 'The truth is that this whole way of thinking is wrong, and if such a [supranatural] Being did exist, he would be the very devil.' God is discovered for him only in loving relations between people. At times he almost seems to say that love is God, or at least that human love brings God into existence. But he too finds a transcendental element in life. He writes: 'For it is an integral part of [Freud's] argument that fantasies about spiritual forces in the occult world are really "projections" or "displacements" of elements in our experience of personal relationships which we seek to avoid recognizing, but it is hard to see why the common projections made by the human race should have a numinous, transcendental character unless there is something numinous and transcendental in the experience of personal relationships themselves.'[3] He has not only argued for the existence of something numinous and transcendental in the experience of personal relationships themselves but even that this brought him into the Church of England. Just as Tillich argues for a transcendence in depth, so Wren-Lewis argues for a transcendental experience of the other. His arguments resemble

Buber's claim that in the full and complete encounter of an I with a Thou, the Divine Thou is encountered also. Of course, this is rather to use 'transcendence' in the first *Oxford English Dictionary* sense—of transcending as the process of rising above or surmounting [something else]. The argument which we cannot understand, the music which baffles us, the good book we find unreadable—these transcend us in that they are beyond our reach. The moral value we accept but do not act upon could be argued to transcend us. Perhaps every valuation—in the sense that it is a judgment upon situations—transcends the facts it assesses. The whole existentialist conception of the 'other'—as one who sees me, defines me, judges me, condemns me, disorients me—is an argument for the discovery of the transcendent in the encounter with other persons on the completely human plane. In making it, Sartre refused to divinize transcendence, it is important to note.

As one would expect of a follower of Bultmann, this point of view is very much part of Ronald Gregor Smith's restoration of the transcendent to the Christian scheme.

'The reality of transcendence is not properly comprehended in terms of a metaphysical postulating of substances, or of two worlds, or of two heterogeneous entities. But the reality of transcendence is experienced as an event which happens to us. We are confronted by the other. Here in time and space, in the midst of our temporal history, in our very historicity, and constituting that historicity, we are faced by the other. The reality of transcendence encounters us when we are aware of the presence of another centre of will and of personal being. It is the otherness of the human other, of the other I, the I who is a Thou to me, and to whom I in turn am a Thou, in mutuality of historical existence, which constitutes the actuality of transcendence. Transcendence is thus not a reality separate from us, but is the way in which we express the historical reality of encounter with others. Transcendence is not an entity with a separate being of its own, but is the way in which being is: namely, in relation with others. This relation is thus an action, not a state: it is the act or venture of mutual existence.

'In an analogous way, we suggest, we may speak of the relation with God. His transcendence, too, is the expression for the historical reality of his encounter with his creatures. The way in which he is therefore always *in actu*: it is a way of movement, a dynamic personal being-for-us. God's being is thus relational through and through.'[4]

In the writers I have quoted, these experiences—the discovery of transcendence in situations, in love, in encounter with the other, in meeting with the Jesus of history, in social and historical realities—are somehow held tangentially to point to God or in some special sense to an experience of God, or perhaps as some would argue to the only possible experience of God.

One respects the striving for honesty as well as for a rich and complex understanding of the true nature of religious demands upon man they show. But one has to ask does this alternative transcendence succeed where the more precise but more primitive notion perhaps has failed, or is argued to have done so?

Spiritual and workaday transcendence

I think a linguistic critique, following upon the lines of Paul van Buren, could succeed in showing that empirical man is not necessarily more moved or convinced by an oblique and shadowy evocation of God through certain human experiences than by the direct statements of the creeds. It could be argued too, I think, that two experiences are being taken together in this secularized transcendence—the workaday problems of human encounter and communication (Sartre) and the mystery and even awe that the existence of other beings promotes in us. When we reflect on them they appear unfathomable, inalienable, alien. In other human beings we encounter alternative wills to our own, alternative centres of the universe; we both need and fear them. This is what Wren-Lewis means by his numinous and transcendent experience of others. But then *all* being is mysterious, not simply human being. To link that being in its ground or creation with God because of this mystery is to bring back through the window the transcendence thrown out of the door. The linguistic analyst might argue that for the workaday experience one does not need the God-hypothesis, and alternatively, that a sense of mystery or inadequacy before existence does not automatically justify the use of the word 'God', particularly if its previously accepted content is rejected. What was now the content of the word God, he might ask, that it could be used as an explanation for the mystery? This would be a fair question. Has it really been answered?

Then I would say myself two things—first, that loving en-

D

counters between persons are not all of one piece, they cover an extraordinary variety of situations from frenzied personal relations, full of suffering, to the stern demands of justice (in saying 'God is love' perhaps one has also to say what *sort* of love—and here the categories *eros, philia, agape* are probably not enough); second, that many human encounters are contests of wills or of understanding, and some, as real as the encounters of love, and as formative, are hard personal encounters with fanaticism, violence of mind, emotional aggression, blindness, positive evil. What precisely is their role in the discovery of God 'in the accessible neighbour who is given to us again and again', as Bonhoeffer said? The same questions pose themselves to me in the discovery of God in the social and historical order. How do we discriminate? What criteria are we now invited to use? If God is to be discovered in personal and social contexts only, as so many American radical theologians appear to argue, what is the role and significance of the evil discovered there too?

A middle way?

I notice that John Robinson claims that there is a middle way between supranaturalism and naturalism. The naturalist critique which tore down the supranaturalist idol was correct, he argues, but it is wrong when it claims that the word God is 'merely a redundant name for nature or humanity'. And I note that Tillich says that the finite world points *beyond* itself, that is it is self-transcendent, and from all that he has said in so many eloquent works it points to the God of whom he wrote among other things, 'Only God can forgive, because in Him alone love and justice are completely united.' Perhaps one ought not to complain if he refuses the term 'being' or 'existence' to the Divine Person he discovers, but I cannot resist the notion that this Divine Person is sometimes accepted in his separation and transcendence and sometimes not. For myself, I do not think that the new limited transcendence, or self-transcendence, or ek-stasis, can be sustained as a doctrine unless in some sense God is granted reality and existence independent of man. The finite world Tillich says points beyond itself. But if there is only the finite world, then it points at nothing. If it points to an infinite and eternal world, then Christian dualism is back again and God with us again as the external judge or saviour.

The death of God

It would seem that the new school of 'Death of God' theologians in America carry even further the reductionist work of the new theologians we have glanced at. Paul van Buren, of course, in *The Secular Meaning of the Gospel*, comes close to a Christian atheism, as we have seen, in that the term 'God' can be dispensed with, he asserts, and notions of divine transcendence abandoned as meaningless. He rests both faith and doctrines of the church on the secularized Jesus—the man whose freedom from human tyrannies of thought, custom, censure, bigotry, hatred was so complete that his morally redeemed humanity was contagious for others. The instruments of van Buren's demolition of traditional Christian positions are logical positivism and linguistic analysis, which he accepts far too uncritically, failing to ask in what sense they are vulnerable in themselves, or for the purposes he had in mind, or for philosophical tasks generally. It is arguable that the poverty of his instruments is responsible for the poverty of his results.

There are two others whose teachings require comment, William Hamilton and Thomas J. Altizer. They are both only at the beginning of their self-appointed tasks. The starting-point for both of them is what this short book is all about—the crisis for the churches, but more especially the theological crisis. Not simply, however, the loss of a felt sense of the transcendent, in Ronald Gregor Smith's phrase, but of meaning ascribable to the word 'God'. Their starting-point is first of all *cultural*. Our technological culture is not one which sits and waits upon answers to prayers. There is no problem to which solution is necessary which is not regarded at least as *ultimately* soluble by the application of human intelligence.[5] In the search for solutions God is not simply an unnecessary, but an unwelcome hypothesis. Every neophyte in theology is familiar with this assessment of the cultural crisis for the faith. But it is one thing to see that Christian doctrine and worldly views are as oil and water. It is another thing to argue that the worldly doctrine is correct for theology. In one place, *The New Essence of Christianity*, Hamilton speaks, as it were within the ethos of contemporary culture, of the inevitable suspicion the Christian has 'that God himself has withdrawn'. 'Those of us who are trying to make the Christian faith intelligible to ourselves and to others have probably spent too much time and too many words saying that we saw and believed what we did not truly see and believe, and we did not like the experience of having deceived ourselves, even if we deceived no one else' (pp. 28–9). The unbelieving world, he somewhere remarks, in his compassionate, reflective work, 'has come to rest within ourselves', and our faith is reduced to fragments, partial vision, broken speech, because of this. He is fighting against the style of thought 'which believes that Christianity must always be on the offensive'. Theology today is like living in a house with six storm windows to cover eight windows. And we might add, in winter. William Hamilton's faith is a faith for a wintry day. At a crucial point in his argument in *The New Essence of Christianity* he writes, 'I am not here referring to a belief in the non-existence of God. I am talking about a growing sense, in both non-Christians and Christians, that God has withdrawn, that he is absent, even that he is somehow dead.'

What is left is Jesus the Lord, but Jesus in his suffering and desolation—'he was despised and rejected of men'. It is the lordship alone of the suffering servant he will accept, and the modern Christian's style of life is to stand with the suffering God in the midst of a godless world, and in the end with more resignation than rebellion.

Hamilton's faith has perhaps become more wintry still since *The New Essence of Christianity*. According to Ogletree, in an autobiographical essay Hamilton argued that the theologian today 'doesn't believe in God, whatever that means, or that there is *a* God, or that God *exists*'. The implication is that an awkward cultural development for Christianity has been transformed into a *necessary* theological proposition. For Hamilton now, Thomas Ogletree says in *The 'Death-of-God' Controversy*, it has become theologically definitive: 'Hamilton's most recent statements about the "death of God" are more unqualified. Apparently the sense of waiting and even tentative hope of a new kind of awareness of God are surrendered altogether. As he puts it, the experiences of "God" which we still have can more usefully be re-described or re-named; as for the rest they are simply no longer part of our lives.'[6] The sacred belongs only to human experiences such as birth, love and death.

Thomas Altizer interprets the 'death of God' altogether in Hegelian fashion. Like Harvey Cox, he sees the present cultural discovery of the missing God as divinely intended in the act of incarnation—God *meant* to free man from subjection to a despotic divine Otherness—but it is only now, at the point of historical fulfilment, Christianly acceptable.

The Hegelian dialectic moves from thesis to antithesis, to synthesis, which is then the form of still another thesis. It is a doctrine of eternal flux, but flux subject to inner law by which the contradictions within a given state of affairs drive it on, towards its opposite. In fact, every state of affairs is incomplete, and the law of its drive towards its opposite is the law of its drive towards completion, towards fulfilment. Altizer discovers in the 'deity' of oriental mysticism the precise dialectical opposite of Christian profanity. The oriental totality of being with which the eastern mystic seeks communion is, rather like the perfection of a Platonic other-world, still and harmonious and complete. It is everything that a dynamic world of process, change and decay is not. If we contrast the world in which Christ moved with the world of perfect platonic God we see Altizer's point. Incarnation means that God *empties* himself into the world. The Word becomes flesh. But not simply that God in the form of Jesus came into the world, then went away again, leaving a 'message', a 'revelation', behind him, but that God *stayed* in the world, incarnated in the world, emptied into the world, losing in the process his identity as remote and inaccessible and perfect Other. The meaning of this for Altizer is that a real, irreversible Hegelian movement has taken place. The quiescent, perfect, transcendent God was negated; he moved over into his opposite, the active, immanent God of a world of change. Transcendence was abandoned. The Incarnation became the on-going event which Teilhard de Chardin in his way also celebrates. Yet the 'death of God' in Altizer is not quite as radical as it appears at first sight. God changes his form in the kenotic process of pouring himself into his world. It is God willing his own 'death' by willing not to be separate from his creation.

Le trahison des clercs

Of course, the questions are endless. This form of process theology finds the person of Jesus inconvenient. He is acceptable as a symbol of incarnation, but not appreciated as an intruding person at the awkward actual moment at which it happens in history. Process theology is better developed, as Whitehead develops it, outside the Christian frame of reference.

Then, too, a purely immanentist religion has, like nineteenth century idealism, difficulty in finding anything bad or evil. If God is so emptied into the world that he is not to be separated from it, whence comes all that is perverse, destructive and the cause of suffering and in any case whence comes our right to *criticize* it or *condemn* it? In terms of process, present evil is the instrument of future good: this is implicit in all ideas of a worldly evolution. If God, on the other hand, is so emptied into the world that God is *not,* but the world is, then the world is all the God we need. Again by what right do we reject the products, spiritual, social, political, material of the world? Altizer's theology would seem to lead to a world-acceptance of the kind Jesus came into the world to reject.

If, on the other hand, the incarnation of God in the world is a voluntary deed, an act of grace, then God remains master both of himself and of the world. The transformation of the world and reascension of God are both conceivable. If so, the elements of inevitability and irreversibility we find in Altizer—and in Hegel, and for that matter in Teilhard de Chardin too—are lost. The divine options are still open. But if the Word *cannot* be withdrawn, divine freedom is gone and a process, a dialectic, is master both of God and the world, just as with Whitehead it was creativity rather than God which ruled. Despite the deep spirituality of Altizer's writings, one fears that one result of the acceptance of his theology would be the enthronement of an arid process over the world. But the modern world has only just escaped—and even then only in the west—from being 'processed' by theories of historical inevitability associated with Karl Marx, Hegel, Nietzsche, Spengler, Comte, with all those appalling and destructive consequences it is now theologically fashionable to ignore yet which in their day—which is our day —did such destruction to European civilization that it may never culturally recover from it. It would be a tragic consummation of Christianity if Christians now urged, under plea of the death of God, a new sort of evolutionary positivism on the world. That would be the final *trahison des clercs.*

The experience of God standing over the world, God concerned and seeking human acknowledgment, and suffering with man, the very God of Christian encounter, has affected history in an irrevocable sense. By such a God man was called out of himself, by him brought to a redemption he could not achieve himself, enabled to see himself in all his coarseness and brutality, to see that *something* stood in eternal vigilance, eternal judgment over what he did with his life on earth. It was the denial of that God, the rebellion against him, that robbed the world of absolute standards—if God is not, everything is possible and permitted—genocide and concentration camps and political terror—that terrible war against man which man at this moment wages with endless ferocity. At least let us record *this* product of our history as part of the achievement of man's coming-of-age. 'Man distils evil as a bee distils honey,' William Golding wrote, and Berdyaev said, 'It is not man who wants to be human, but God who calls him to be human.' God in fact was the humanly incorruptible who down the ages saved man's humanity even against man's will. Perhaps that modern humility Hamilton praises so highly ought to warn us against celebrating the death of God *christianly*. It often used to be said of conquerors that they in turn were conquered by the culture of those they conquered. I suspect this is happening today. The West by an exhausting military effort destroyed Hitler, by a long spiritual effort fended off communism, but now the cultural values of Stalin, Hitler and de Sade master us. Behind the technological façade the most desolating and destructive doctrine of man grows up—that finally he is an expendable scrap, a nothing, which no one values, least of all man himself. The final irony would be for Christian theologians—ignorant of, or insensitive in their ivory towers to, recent history—to bless this degradation with a Christian blessing.

What, after all, keeps the 'death-of-God' theologians even able to speak of themselves as theologians is, in the event, their Christologies. For all of them Jesus is in some sense Lord, or in Blake's sense 'God *is* Jesus'. He appears to represent for all of them an absolute event, an unconditional judgment on the world, a point of total change in human consciousness. In some sense all of them would argue that the duty of his followers must be in terms of the struggle for social justice, for loving personal relations, for racial and national reconciliations, for new insights in sexual relations and individual liberty. Almost, the old social gospel of Christianity which argued that Christians had a special duty to be involved in the social struggle has

been turned upside down. Now it is almost sufficient to say that
if one is engaged in the social struggle that is all that is involved
in fulfilling the commands of Jesus. But by what mental *tour de
force* the lordship of Jesus over the world can be insisted upon
when the transcendental frame which sustained and satisfied
him is abandoned I would not know. For my own part it was
never Jesus who validated the deity, but a doctrine of the deity
which validated—made sense of—his life and passion.

Enough has been said to reveal the depth and extent of the
contemporary theological ferment which threatens the whole of
the received theological structure of the Christian churches.
Finally, I would argue, the totality of social and intellectual
pressures crystallizes into one theological issue—does any meaning still attach to historical Christian claims? Do we have therefore to speak not only of the death of God but also of the death
of the church in the hearts of men preparatory to its death as an
institution in the world?

CHAPTER EIGHT

THE RENEWAL OF THE CHURCH

Renewal of worship

An issue of *Paris Match* just prior to Christmas 1966 contained an illustrated account, '*La Nouvelle Messe*', of liturgical innovations inspired by priests and laity of the Roman Church on the continent. One report described a mass celebrated as though it were the last supper with a priest without liturgical garments at a table with some sixteen grammar school boys. The priest blessed the wine and bread and himself communicated. The bread and wine were passed round to everyone to partake. Then, after last prayers, a meal was eaten in all the noise and good fellowship of an ordinary repast. This took place in Holland. In a more orthodox mass in Flemish-speaking Belgium, the communicants received the wafer in their hands. Among them were those who had complained that it was 'babyish' to have it placed on the lips. In the parish of St. Anthony in Nimèque the mass was sung to 'beat music'. '*Dans une petite maison, en pays flamand, six jeunes hommes sont réunis autour d'une table couverte d'un simple tissue de laine gris. Ensemble, dans le plus extrême dépouillement, ils célèbrent l'eucharistie, C'est une véritable liturgie qui se déroule. Le prêtre lit une épître de saint Paul et un passage d'un evangeliste. Tous chantent des cantiques en néerlandais. Puis ils font une courte méditation, après avoir écouté une homilie. Alors, dans le plus grand silence, le prêtre consacre le pain et le vin. Dans un intense recueillement, chacun se communie.*'[1] The photographs show the communion bread not in the form of wafers, but of flat bread or girdle cake, and of worshippers 'communicating themselves', seated before the table, and in both bread and wine.

Yet another beautifully illustrated double-page spread shows twenty or so Catholic and Protestant students of Utrecht taking part, seated at table, in a eucharistic meal. The bread—unleavened bread, '*pain azyme*'—has been consecrated. The slices are passed round in baskets. The wine is consecrated in ordinary carafes and drunk throughout the meal.[2] The students are members of a movement called *Shalom* (the Hebrew word for peace), and their intention is to attend at a mass where they will do '*ce qu'a fait le Christ à la dernière Cène*'. The report moved on to Africans who beat drums and dance to them before altars at which the mass is being celebrated, and to nuns in Brazil who, in the absence of priests, distribute the host. The reaction of the Vatican to this publicity was very sharp. The liturgy was being desecrated. 'For some time, several newspapers and magazines have offered to their readers news and photographs of liturgical ceremonies, above all eucharistic celebrations, that are alien to the Catholic religion, almost improbable, such as family communions celebrated in private homes, followed by meals, Masses with unusual and arbitrary rites, and sometimes accompanied by music of a totally profane and worldly character that is not worthy of a sacred act.' It all had to stop.

While it is certain that *Paris-Match* exaggerated the extent of the irregularities, the interesting thing is that they happen at all on the scale which approaches a movement. Nothing comparable has taken place in the Church of England, except here and there special services of young people to rock-and-roll or beat or pop music, and some experimental eucharists using jazzy music with episcopal authority. House-communions, again under approval, have been a familiar feature of the liturgical movement, but in them the liturgy and practice have not differed seriously from the services either of 1662 or 1928. There is nothing revolutionary in them. If anything they are a cross between eucharists said in private chapels and the well-established practice of sick communions. The two great liturgical questions which have agitated the Church of England have been whether the traditional Sunday pattern of early communion, eleven o'clock mattins and six-thirty evensong, should be dropped in favour of parish communion for everybody as the main Sunday service, and whether the services themselves should be revised and modernized! The victory is to both these movements. Except in extreme evangelical churches, or old-fashioned broad churches, the Parish Communion is in favour. And the 1662 services are being or have been revised, and experiment in them has Parliamentary approval.

It is interesting that Church of England members have so long and so supinely submitted to state control of worship. It was, naturally enough, Henry VIII who first began to legislate a liturgy. The young Edward VI, or his council, gave us the prayer books of Cranmer of 1549 and 1552. Elizabeth I revised the 1552 book in 1559. Finally, the 1662 Act of Uniformity established rigid liturgical orthodoxy in the Book of Common Prayer which has been obligatory ever since. It is still largely Cranmer's book and, as some modern theologians have protested, obsessive with his sense of guilt and unworthiness, and thin on joy. Its English is sublime and it has stood up remarkably to the test of time, but it is also sometimes rotund and diffuse, masking in rolling phrases the acid of Christian judgment upon man and society—save perhaps in the service of commination, where the triumphalist denunciations call down the wrath of God upon those who reject the authority of the church. (In this service the church most clearly appears in its punitive juridico-political role.)

As Professor Kilpatrick tells us in *Remaking the Liturgy*, in the nineteenth century the 1662 Prayer Book was being 'rigorously interpreted' as a Common Law document, as though worship was a copyright affair and one involved oneself in breaches of the law if one did not reproduce the copyrighted material *exactly*. The proposed new Book of Common Prayer, assembled after years of heart searching debate, was rejected by Parliament, the sovereign power, in 1927 and 1928, and 1662 legalism refastened on the church, though farcically, for 1662 was the law no one bothered to obey except in so far as he chose, and the state was without publicly acceptable sanctions to compel anyone to do so.

The Alternative Services, First and Second Series, remain, with sensible changes, within the 1662 ethos. This would seem a proper thing to do only if there has to be a final, rigid form for just about everything. Even so, the Commission which produced them might have been still more radical in its abandonment of ecclesiastical language. But the point is *does worship need to be fixed in an unalterable frame of language and procedures?* What right have we, anyway, to imprison the spiritual responses of future generations in our modes and our words? It seems almost the antithesis of worship that it has to be fixed. One can see the importance of a general pattern to the church's year so that its common worship moves in a uniformity of *attention* from Advent to Advent. One can understand that certain elements of services ought to be common to us all, the Lord's prayer, the creeds, the words of consecration, of blessing and dismissal, and that there should be *recommended* scriptural readings and collects for appropriate days and feasts. But it is essential that, beyond the bare core of acts of worship which we all affirm because they constitute our open confession of common faith, there should be every possible room for spontaneity and experiment in worship. 'The real difficulty,' Professor Kilpatrick has said, 'is to overcome ignorance, sloth, caution, a natural conservatism and timidity, and to revive spontaneity in worship which the emphasis over 400 years on conformity and lawful authority has done so much to choke.'

He recognizes that perhaps eccentrics might have to be checked by decree of the bishop acting with the diocesan synod. All the same, he pleads for a grass-roots growth of freedom in worship in which the liturgical commission would act as 'the chief leader and educator of the church in liturgical matters. It should be competent to give an expert opinion, but much more to act as a clearing house for new developments in liturgy, advising, encouraging and, where necessary, discouraging. It would be up to the commission itself to establish its own moral authority by the wisdom and judgment of its recommendations. Given this, it could co-operate with the parish in a great adventure of recovery and creation.

'This involves trusting the congregations with great responsibility, but they are already entrusted with the issues of spiritual life and death in their parishes. It returns to them some of the initiative which the Christian congregations had in the beginning and which the legislators assumed under Henry VIII and his successors.'[8]

I believe, too, that the church has spiritually impoverished itself by its sole reliance on the canon of scriptures as the prose of its worship (and perhaps vulgarized its worship with some of its hymns). Just as it is a sin against the spirit to imagine that Cranmer's words alone are appropriate to our worship, so it is a sin to suppose that nothing important, religiously speaking, has been written about our faith since the New Testament. There are thousands of sources as profound and illuminating as the scriptures, which Christian congregations never hear, or even hear about, because not of the canon. That selected readings should be made available, as readily as hymns and anthems, to add new dimensions to worship would seem elementary common sense. Why should the voices of Augustine and Benedict, More and Erasmus, Milton and Donne, Luther and Calvin, Péguy and Temple not be heard in the churches in their own right as apostles of the faith? What a change they would be from those incomprehensible Old Testament lessons and vengeful (and now discreetly censored) Psalms!

The breath of reality they would introduce might be brought to bear on the communion service too. No doubt the disciples ate real, if unleavened, bread at the last supper and the cup of wine was meant to sustain them. But the elements of the eucharist have become so symbolic as to be incorporeal, wraithlike—a wafer as near bread as digestible plastic, and the merest smear of wine on the lips. I remember at my first communion as a child, to which I had eagerly looked forward, and for which I had fasted overnight, my sense of being cheated by receiving, hungry and thirsty at eight o'clock in the morning, a few crumbs of bread and the thinnest sip of wine. I have thought ever since that eucharistic participation would be more real and not less holy if one had a less fleeting contact with genuine bread and wine, and if week by week someone in the parish baked that bread for us and bought the Beaujolais where the rest of the wine comes from. A specially marketed *sacramental* wine seems as nonsensical as a special bread, holier than just ordinary *bread*. I am reminded of the priest who preached against exaggerations typical of our times. He said that there was a baker's van which toured his parish advertising a 'Wonderloaf'. 'Just as cheap as ordinary bread', the slogan went. 'But it *is* ordinary bread', the priest told his congregation. By the same token, let our communion bread be ordinary bread and not tarted-up wafers. I can see even more advantages in embodying the eucharistic service in a special, but real meal, the meal of followers of Jesus rather than the ghost of it present at a normal communion of almost any denomination.

The legal forms of churches

The church of the Palestinian mission had no legal form. It was first a group of friends and followers of Jesus drawn by his charismatic power, and at its greatest a cohort of disciples. Loyalty to Jesus and the baptismal sign introduced by John the Baptist kept the followers together. There is evidence, after the

ascension, of a new contractual basis of membership of the
society of the followers of Jesus. The new leader Matthias is
elected by orderly procedures: goods are held in common and
breakers of the rule punished; funds are gathered and help
organized for Christians in need. All clearly is on a voluntary
basis and when a member ceased to believe, nothing (except the
pressure of public opinion or fear of divine retribution perhaps)
could prevent him from leaving: no legal sanctions could be
invoked against him. It was on this voluntary basis that the
early church grew, whether as a free or a proscribed institution.

The Constantine settlement changed everything. It established the position that there was, parallel with the secular
authority, a proper spiritual government, entitled to the support
of the political powers—even financial support—and on its own
part justified in using the secular authorities for its own ends—
the extermination of heretics, the punishment of religious
offenders, the conversion of peoples (as, for example, in St.
Augustine's campaign in England, *cuius regio, eius religio*) and
war against threatening infidels. The climax of this triumphalist
doctrine was the eventual papal assertion not of an equality of
powers but of supremacy—that every secular power drew its
authority from the pope as the vicar of Christ.

Only slowly has the church (and chiefly as a result of internal
dissension) come to understand what kind of a prison it succeeded in making for itself by the legal forms which bound it to
society and made it possible to preach the Christian gospel by
threats. Above all, it was the Reformation which slowly sun-
dered church from society. Where there was a plurality of sects,
which ought even an avowedly Christian society to support?
Where the choice was all or none, the decision usually was none.
Even so, certain legal forms lived on, such as church taxes in
Germany or the general recognition of church educational
rights. The Puritan New England settlements, Knox's Presby-
terianism and Calvin's Geneva sought to establish Protestant
theocratic government.

In England, despite the failure to maintain uniformity
(sought for political as much as for religious reasons), legally
'prescribed' religion lived on in the established church con-
trolled by Parliament and under the supremacy of the crown,
regardless of the presence of many parallel 'unestablished' de-

nominations and sects, of the freely proselytizing Roman Church, and a disestablished Church of Wales and a differently established Church of Scotland. But the legal forms which make the Church of England the specially favoured son of the state also prohibit it from reaching its majority, 'coming of age', getting the key of its own front door.

The other great force sundering church and state was the political revolution of the eighteenth century. One could not press the rights of man—freedom of speech and assembly, equal justice, representative assemblies—and denounce the special privilege of autocracy and monarchy, without at the same time proclaiming freedom of conscience and of religious belief and protesting against religious privileges. The situation in France before the Revolution in which the church was a state within a state had become intolerable. The completely secularized state and civil structures of France and the United States were the revolutionary consequence. Their establishment was held to be a major victory for humanity: the major churches today would recognize this despite their bitter opposition to the loss of privilege in the past, as the Vatican's council's resolution on freedom of religion demonstrates. Of the Christian nations of Europe only backward Spain believes that the nations can prescribe one faith and proscribe another, though communist states continue the inquisitional evil of dictating secular 'religious' beliefs to the populace.

In a short and learned book, *The One-sided Reciprocity*, Professor Peter Hinchliff traces the relationship of church and state in England from the first unselfconscious partnership of the early middle ages to the 'managed' relationship between church and state in the later medieval period—a managed relationship not unlike that between the Labour government and the trade unions at the present moment—with the trade unions free and self-governing as the medieval church was, but the government now as then having the 'edge' because of its ability to legislate and to resort to force. The murder of Thomas à Beckett is indicative of the tensions of the situation; but it tells us so much of the relative roles of church and state even then, that it never occurs to us to wonder if instead of knights murdering an archbishop monks might have been assassinating a king.

'But,' Hinchliff writes, 'from the second chapter on we have been considering a deliberate and selfconscious attempt to create a relationship, enshrined in legislation, which was advertised as being in theory an equal partnership. In creating this partnership the state took the initiative. It has become a commonplace to say that, whatever else the reformation in England may have been, it was an act of state. And once the state had acted in this fashion [invoking legal sanctions against all who resisted, we might add], the projected partnership ceased to exist ... after 1559 Parliament could, but Convocation could not, undo or alter the settlement' (p. 215).

This admirable book details some of the consequences of this spiritual and political disaster for the Church of England. 'There was no opportunity for the Church, even through the clergy, to have a say in the choice of bishops. Discipline became chaotic and haphazard and an easy target for the derision of outsiders. Revision of liturgy and canon law became cumbersome and almost impossible in practice. Even well-meaning attempts to allow the church to have some freedom to legislate for itself only succeeded in making the machinery more cumbersome still without guaranteeing any real liberty—Above all the other difficulties created by the establishment is the difficulty of knowing exactly what the true position of the established church is. This is a direct consequence of its being established *by law*—not by *a* law, but by law ... it is virtually impossible to know what the law is without litigation, lengthy enquiry or a process of trial and error' (pp. 216–17).

Apart from the humiliations suffered by the church, so that even its minor posts as well as its major ones can be distributed by outside parties (something on the pattern of the American 'spoils' system) there are the insufferable delays imposed upon it by tortuous legal processes. Everyone is familiar with the fate of the 1928–9 prayer book, but even so good a measure as the Pastoral Measure passed by Church Assembly in July 1967 promises endless opportunities for delay. A scheme for a necessary parochial reorganization drawn up by a diocesan pastoral committee and approved by the Bishop has to go to the Church Commissioners for approval or amendment. (The Church Commissioners basically constitute the department of state for the legal and financial control of the church.) From them the scheme must be submitted to 'Her Majesty in Council' for approval. If, however, it declares churches redundant it must be submitted to parochial church councils concerned and other interested parties, be published in local newspapers and so on. Notice of appeal against a scheme may be lodged with the Clerk of Privy Council, and this can be heard by the Judicial Committee of the Privy Council, which in its turn can recommend that the scheme be accepted, rejected or sent back for reconsideration. If the last, everything begins again, or all is abandoned in despair, no matter how important. The possibilities of delay are endless, their spiritual cost is cruel. The mere rectification of parish boundaries could in theory go up to the highest secular legal authority in the land for decision. I dare not compute the burden of legal costs the church so innocently bears. What powers of reform the Pastoral Measure gives with one hand, the legal delays take away with the other!

By contrast, Canon Bernard Pawley, writing of the Roman Church in France (in *The Church Times* of 21 April 1967) says:

'To deal with a situation which is pathetically parallel to our own (an average of 700 ordinations in 1955–9 dropped to 570 for 1960–4; and a gross maldistribution of clergy between dioceses) the bishops set up what is clearly a French edition of the Paul Report Commission, though deployment will not be coupled with pay nor again will the complication of state and party trusts be a difficulty. The equivalent of our "problem of the South-East" seems to have been solved with a few strokes of the pen by the creation of five new dioceses in the Paris area. Once again the absence of legal encumbrances has made the task incomparably easier.'

Even the ponderous juridico-political structure of the Church of Rome can move faster to grapple with mission situations than the Church of England, tangled as it is in the legal leading-strings of establishment.

When the bishops and archbishops of the Anglican communion assemble at Lambeth in 1968 they will all, with one exception, represent self-governing churches. That exception is the venerable, historic institution from which they sprang, and which claims to lead them.

Ecumenism

In *Religion in Secular Society*, Bryan Wilson makes a critique of what he calls 'ecumenicalism'. His case is simple. The churches are growing weaker, therefore they tend to grow closer together. Churches do not unite when they are strong. As they grow weaker their doctrinal differences appear less important. It becomes easier therefore to unite. In any case the sharp differences which drive people to break away from a mother church and to form sects or denominations grow blunter with passing generations and lose their meaning, and the puzzle comes to discover what was the force in them which drove people apart originally.

Bryan Wilson also argues that unity is in the professional interest of various ministries. 'Ecumenicalism' he judges on the whole to be a professional (ministerial) enterprise promoted very much out of self-interest. This analysis is confidently argued. Following Wilson, one analogy would seem to be with businesses, where the failing enterprise sells out to the strong one in order to save its assets, to protect the interests of its promoters and the livelihood of its employees. But this is the capitulation of weakness to strength, and what Bryan Wilson is really affirming is the existence of a common weakness in all western faiths. Bankrupt businesses do not unite—the pooling of many weaknesses does not add up to a collective strength, but to even more insoluble dilemmas on the whole. A more satisfactory analogy might be the re-uniting of scattered military forces in order that a regrouped army might re-discover its collective strength. This might more nearly accord with the situation of Christian churches. The trouble with the application of that analogy to Bryan Wilson's argument is that here the weakness is brought about by division, *not by decline*, and that unity exposes again the previously concealed strength. Another analogy of this kind might be the gathering of weak, scattered colleges together to form a strong university. The early church was much more aware than Reformation Christianity of the dangers of doctrinal and organizational disunity.

Bryan Wilson's argument about weakness could still be totally true, and miss the point. The point for the Christian is not whether unity is expedient but whether it is right or wrong. The Wilson analysis seems to miss out a whole historical continuum, as for instance that no one in the first stages of the Reformation wanted the atomization of the Christian church into sects and denominations, but just its reform. It took a long time for the dismembered Church to work through the consequences of the

Reformation (and the 'real-politik' alignments with the secular authorities which ensued), but there was always one fixed point in that process—the teachings of the Founder, inevitably alien to disunity and hostility between his followers. In other words, certain spiritual values in Christianity stood constantly in judgment over *the convenience and self-interest of disunity*.

Moreover, the modern drive to 'ecumenicalism' came out of mission field *expansion*, not contraction, when the absurdity, doctrinally as well as organizationally, of dividing tribes in the bush into Methodists, Baptists, Anglicans, Peculiar People was brought home to missionaries (often laymen) steeped in sectarian divisions which in a new continent suffered 'a sea-change into something rich and rare'. And two great laymen, Mott and Oldham, played the greatest part in initiating the ecumenical drive (against official indifference), and the conference where it all began, the World Missionary Conference at Edinburgh in 1910, was at a period when the success and permanency of Christian churches in the world were not seriously in question. Historically, too, it has been a lay élite which has always had difficulty in swallowing carefully preserved ministerial views of the propriety of doctrinal differences, and it was with the laity not the ministries that the whole modern ecumenical movement began.

No, historically speaking, a Marxist analysis might be more valuable than the sociological critique which Bryan Wilson makes. And it might be this—that the whole drive of denominationalism and sectarian experiment to which the Reformation gave rise has burnt itself out at the centre and flickers on only at the fringes. An historical movement has exhausted all its possibilities, and it is perhaps not without significance that the rise of denominationalism corresponded with the rise of the bourgeoisie and its decline with the bourgeois collapse. Far from a purified and exalted Christianity arising from all that zeal, that fury of cross-sect denunciation, what emerges is the bankruptcy of separatism. The movement had within it the seeds of its own destruction. Yet *Christianity* remains, and ecumenism is the product of the discovery that what unites Christians is more important than what divides them—or, if that is too absolute a statement as yet, *ought to be more* important.

What the Edinburgh Conference began to set in motion was

the drawing together of the Protestant churches and denominations, of which the outcome was the World Council of Churches (with its national and local councils). For nearly half a century after Edinburgh the Roman Church remained aloof from ecumenical moves: its official position was that there was only one true Church, 'separated brethren' were in error, in apostasy; let them recant their error and return to the true obedience and Christianity would be united. Basically, as there was only the one church, it could not be divided. Roman Catholicism remained as shut away (officially) as Stalin's Russia. The result was a nervous polarization, Romans round the pope, Protestants round the World Council of Churches. Not that the latter, a weak, federal, consultative structure, ever resembled the authoritarian structure of Rome. But it did look as though the drive to reunion might freeze Christians in three historical positions—the Roman, the Orthodox, the Protestant—between which the gaps would widen. This was not a development likely to attract the Church of England, which argued itself to be both Catholic and Reformed, and the high church wing of which tended always to be more Romish than the Romans. The work of Pope John XXIII and of the Vatican Council he promoted has changed the ecumenical scene so radically that it is now possible to see *all* the major churches of the world brought together in some ecumenical relation. But the moment of the visualization of this corresponds with a loosening of the juridico-political structure of Rome itself. It is losing the totalitarian appearance—the fortress under iron discipline over against the world—it has so long presented to those outside. A powerful self-criticism has grown up within it. The centrifugal forces are considerable, and Romans in new countries, rising continents, do not want to be seen, or thought of, as Italian puppets. A federal, rather than a totalitarian, structure would seem inevitable for Rome, with councils of bishops rather than an Italian ecclesiastical bureaucracy as the masters of policy.

Though churches will unite, as it seems reasonably certain Anglicans and Methodists will, and as Presbyterians and Congregationalists are about to, and even new churches will be founded on the dissolution of old, as in the Church of South India, the central problem remains—how are the major churches to be brought together so that there is one world Christian communion? Subservience to one centre is out. The dissolution of all that is unique and individual in separate churches in favour of some flat 'instant' innocuous Christian worship might be a disaster. Several steps appear to be needed: They are—

1. The necessity to maintain the struggle for the union of churches which are close together in history and doctrine (Anglicans and Methodists) or which face a common problem (South India).

2. The continuation of dialogue and consultation between major churches at the highest possible level in order that there might be at the end a world deliberative assembly based on all churches.

3. The encouragement of grass-roots ecumenism.

4. The widening of inter-communion.

Perhaps what one is saying echoes Charles Davis's plea for a new Christian presence in the world. It must be already clear that such a presence cannot be juridico-political in the old triumphalist Roman sense, nor legal-proprietorial in the Church of England sense. Whatever sustenance the new presence derives from the older forms, it must be a humbler, servant form of the Church, ready to suffer and to efface itself, which emerges, and one in which spontaneities of a local and individual character enter into its liturgical and pastoral life. In it, the rush of the Holy Spirit would count for more than the legal barriers between Christians. No one knows what form or forms will emerge. What must prevail among us all is a patient and expectant spirit.

One gets the impression that such an ecumenical grass-roots movement is already on the march on the continent of Europe and that Romans are prominent in it. It is not impossible here. As I was engaged in writing this a Report reached me from a group of clergy from four denominations concerned with Corby New Town. The Ecumenical Study group responsible for the Report, 'began with the conviction that the churches could no longer afford—either in money, manpower, or on grounds of scandal—to act independently in newly developing areas. Just as industry and secular government want to deal with "The Church" and not with many churches so we believe that people making a new life in a new area want to face one call and not many.' The basic demand of the Report is 'for *a single Christian congregation* with one main centre, sponsored by several major denominations'. The central act of worship of the united congregation would be the eucharist and the preaching of the Word. There would be one building. New members would be admitted by a form of invitation—baptism, public profession of faith, laying-on of hands by an Anglican bishop and team members, special prayers and holy communion.[4]

If this came about, here in one new town, under Anglican, Methodist, Congregationalist and Baptist sponsorship, and led by their ministers and laymen, the original Christian congregations of the first century would be restored, an event of tremendous significance. If the continental grass-roots movement already described is a guide it is not impossible to conceive that the Romans would join it at some future time.

The deep church

Finally, the church—the whole church—is not an association of moral improvers, or a society of friends meeting for worship in a particular way, or a club of life-rejectors, or a suburban commuter's conformist paradise, or a refuge for the old and unhappy, or a cult of incense burners or even a society for the preservation of ancient buildings. It is not summed up by any of the pejorative descriptions which come with such facility to us all. It may fulfil all the functions described above and yet not be exhausted by them. It may fulfil few of them, yet still be the church. For the church fundamentally, finally, is an assertion about the nature of man and an assertion about the nature of God, and of the relation between them and the collective orientation of life and witness which flows from these acts of faith. Even so resolutely empirical a reduction of Christianity as R. B. Braithwaite's *An Empiricist's View of the Nature of Religious Belief* comes to rest at the end on a life-orientation determined in the light of the whole Christian story. And the church is not, of course, just what it happens to be at this cross-section of time. It is also the church of history, the church moving through time. The church is its history, and its reflections on its history.

The church does not make a single assertion about God. It does not simply say *Jesus*: or with Blake, 'God is Jesus'. Of course, Christianity is Christocentric. If Jesus be not risen from the dead, Paul said, then is our work in vain. He might have said, if Jesus be not divine, then is our teaching untrue. But the divinity of Jesus was never the single assertion of Christianity, as Christian secularists are tempted to argue today. Jesus never maintained that he alone constituted the source of truth and of holiness: his mission was validated for him because the Father who was in heaven sent him. The priorities have to be understood. It was not the mission of Jesus which validated the existence of God, but the existence of God which illuminated and confirmed the mission of Jesus. No amount of demythologizing or secularizing can remove the dependence of Jesus on the Lord God who was the author of his mission. The early church struggled with the revelation not just of the existence but of the activity of God which this revealed, and enshrined it immortally in the doctrine of the Trinity.

To negate these propositions is to make the life and passion of Jesus meaningless. Jesus cries to God in the garden of Gethsemane, and from the cross. His mission is necessary because men have failed in obedience to, and love of, God. Gamaliel says that if this work be of God, then it will succeed, if not...! Besides, if Christianity was saying that all we know of God is from, or in, Jesus, what sense could it possibly make of the centuries of theocentric Judaism? The Christians embodied the Judaistic scriptures in their own canon and accepted their creation story. If they had said God *is* Jesus, or Jesus is all the God we can ever know, they would have been under strict compulsion to allow that troubled theocentric Jewish history to recede into the darkness. It would have been incomprehensible. Christianity of that sort could scarcely be argued to be a fulfilment of Jewish history, but rather a denial of it.

Set in the frame of man's total religious consciousness, Jewish and Gentile, the life and passion of Jesus is magnificent, terrible. Related as a solitary episode out of the Judaistic context, the one flash illuminating a total darkness, it is the event only of which Schweitzer speaks, of Jesus, a self-deceived Jesus, throwing himself on the wheel of history and being broken by it. If Jesus is all, is man, and no other form of God, no transcendent God exists, then the total religious experience of man is narrowed down to the possibilities which emerge from the three-year mission of Jesus two thousand years ago. Such a secular assertion makes it impossible to conceive of a Jesus in continuing relation, continuing activity in the world after his life, and therefore of the admission of concepts such as continuing grace, redemption, atonement, forgiveness. It is not only that the spiritual dimension of human life is impoverished by its limitation to the lived life of Jesus but that religious creativity goes. We must suck, as the luckless theologians do, on that one poor bone for ever and ever.

The confinement of religious experience to that short humanistic life of Jesus also denies us a natural theology. What are we to say of the meaning of all existence if everything is secularized? Human life is contingent, but what of natural life, of the realm of the inanimate, of the vastity of the cosmos? Is there in these no revelation of God, or the divine? Christians of all centuries down to this—and including this—have sought to say with the Jews that God could be seen revealed in nature and in history, though that did not mean he was, Hegelian fashion, unrolled for human inspection. The mystery, the enigma of God, remained.

The church has to be conceived of as the human reaction to that omnipresent God—transcendent but active, immanent in the human heart, loving and creative, and sustaining the universe. The double orientation of man follows from this discovery. In the world he is meant to be agent and co-partner with God; but his loyalty is not simply to this world, but to the divine creator who set him in the world and who stands beyond it and to whom he is ultimately responsible. These are the human orientations which have made of Christianity the greatest of world religions. (And not to call it a religion is an absurdity, a somewhat hysterical theological reaction to religiosity.)

Finally, let us say that religion is not theology. Religion is the life-experience. Theology is trying to *talk* it, in rather specialized language. Try talking the experience of love in that way, and see where you get. Into something which certainly is not love!

I have sought to say briefly and strongly what I believe to be the irreducible elements of Christianity. It is a faith powerful enough to accept a great deal of demythologizing and theological restatement. But no faith can live on the denial of its past and the rejection of its foundations. The new and pace-making theology is often asking just that. The final crisis for the churches is this—what does Christianity assert as the ultimate and inevitable foundation of its faith? Christianity, I believe, has once again to face its Nicaea.

NOTES

Chapter 1

1 The Salvation Army's story is excitingly told by Richard Collier in *The General Next to God*, London, Collins, 1965.

2 'Like Kingsley, Mr. Colwood loved riding, shooting and fishing, and believed that such sports were congruous with the Christian creed which he unobtrusively accepted and lived up to... One of his maxims was "Don't marry for money but marry where money is", and he had carried this into effect by marrying, when he was over forty, a sensible Scotch lady with a fortune of £1,500 a year, thereby enabling his three sons to be brought up as keen fox-hunters, game-shooters, and salmon-fishers.' *Memoirs of a Fox-Hunting Man*, Siegfried Sassoon, London, Faber, 1937.

3 *The Deployment and Payment of the Clergy*, C.I.O., 1964, and subsequently the Fenton–Morley Report, *Partners in Ministry*, C.I.O., 1967.

4 See especially *A Sociology of English Religion*, David Martin, Heinemann, 1967, and *Religion in a Secular Society*, Bryan Wilson, Watts, 1966, for a guide to the new debate.

Chapter 2

1 David Martin argues for the stability of religious belief and practice in Britain and criticizes facile assumption of decline in *A Sociology of English Religion*, Heinemann, London. 1967. Thomas Ogletree writes, in *Is God Dead?* 'In the United States of America, religion still seems to be booming. The Harris Survey in 1965 indicated that 97 per cent of the population believed in God, and 75 per cent would say that they worship in a church or synagogue at least once a month.'

2 In Toledo in 1965 a truckdriver citizen was honoured because, among many pieces of conspicuous bravery in the course of his life on the roads, he rushed over to an overturned car which had caught fire and rescued the trapped woman driver. 'Whadda yer want to do that for?' one bystander asked, plainly regarding the rescuer as a spoilsport. Another, when asked why he did not help. replied, turning away with a shrug, 'I didn't want to get involved.' The list of these cases is endless, alas. I will conclude it simply by mentioning the affair in England where two young men took two girls away and plied

them experimentally with drugs, then dumped them at a hospital to die, which one of them did.

3 The most brilliant analysis of the conversion of an autonomous rural township into a metropolitan satellite appeared in the *New Yorker* of 7 November 1964, under the title of 'Home Town' by Christopher Rand. It studied the fate of Salisbury, Connecticut.

4 Cf. 'Suicide' by Mary Holland, *The Observer*, 25 June 1967.

5 Cf. in this connexion, 'Civil Religion in America' by Robert N. Bellah, *Daedalus*, Winter 1967.

6 London, Hodder and Stoughton, 1964.

Chapter 3

1 See my *Alternatives to Christian Belief*, Hodder and Stoughton, London, 1967, Chap. 9, 'The Writer and the Human Condition' and *Kenyon Review*, January 1967, the essay by the same title.

2 In *Alternatives to Christian Belief*.

3 *The Observer*, issue of 1 January 1967.

4 See Peter Hinchliff, *The One-Sided Reciprocity*.

Chapter 4

1 *Battersea Deanery Survey*, 1966, the report of a Survey Group under the chairmanship of the Rev. Canon Bazire.

2 *Facts and Figures of the Church of England*, C.I.O., London, 1966, Table 9.

3 See table 29, *Facts and Figures*, 1966. The length of stay in livings was less than five years for half the clergy.

4 *The Deployment and Payment of the Clergy*, C.I.O., 1964, p. 96.

5 See 'Five pointers for the success of the "non-church"' by the Rev. Ray Billington, *The Times*, 19 November 1966.

6 C.I.O., London, 1967.

Chapter 5

1 A Report of the Second Vatican Council.

2 *Further Thinking about the Ministry, 1966*. A symposium issued by the Recruitment Department of A.C.C.M., London, 1966.

3 Cf. *Crisis in the Humanities*, ed. J. H. Plumb, Pelican, London, 1964.

4 It has to be noted that Church of England Advisory Council for the Church's Ministry has recently in agreement with Bishops raised the standards of entry to theological colleges to those normally demanded of universities.

Chapter 6

1 *Komsomolskaya Pravda* (as reported in *The Times*, 25 August 1965) attacks the closing of churches and sterility of the old anti-religious propaganda which 'only strengthens the attraction of religion and breeds the antagonism of the people'. It asks for 'some kind of new ritual which would replace the liturgy of the Church'. 'Why cannot we replace the old ritual with a new one in this epoch when we are transforming the old world into the new and patterning a new social order in place of the old?'

2 For instance, can *all* patterns of behaviour be regarded as institutionalized? Isn't institutionalization a special sort of pattern? Casual or ephemeral patterns like a fashion in clothing or haircuts might be regarded as non-institutionalized. War, race riots and certain forms of mass hysteria are undoubtedly patterns of collective behaviour, but are they institutions? The best definition I know is from the *Oxford Dictionary*: 'an established law, custom, usage, practice, organization or other element in the political or social life of a people'. However, there were good sociological reasons for adopting the simple definition accepted by the consultation: it removed the pejorative associations of the word.

3 *The Reform of Church Government*, Prism Pamphlet No. 20, 1965.

4 The Report of an Archbishop's Committee, *Synodical Government in the Church of England* (C.I.O., 1966) is a great advance and brings nearer the day when the Church establishes one single authority. But in deference to ecclesiastical timidities it leaves shadowy Convocations in existence. And it leaves lay and clerical representation still virtually equal.

Chapter 7

1 David Martin discusses this thoroughly in *Pacifism: an Historical and Sociological Study*, Routledge, London, 1965.

2 Op. cit., pp. 46–7.

3 *The Critical Quarterly*, Spring 1960. I borrow the quotation from *Honest to God*.

4 *Secular Christianity*, pp. 121–2.

5 Theories about the creation or the end of the world or of man can be argued to be strictly unnecessary. They change nothing in man's actual situation.

6 Op. cit., p. 30.

Chapter 8

1 Translation: 'In a little Flemish house six young men came together round a table covered with a plain grey blanket. Together, in the greatest possible simplicity, they celebrated the eucharist. What took place was a genuine liturgy. The priest read an epistle of St. Paul and a lesson from an evangelist. All sang the canticles in Dutch. After listening to a short homily they meditated for a brief space. Then, in profound silence, the priest consecrated the bread and the wine. Then in rapt contemplation, each one took his communion.'

2 I am reminded of the Bishop of Woolwich's 'one meal in the week', usually supper on Saturday, with his wife and children. It arose from 'dissatisfaction with family prayers, with Communion preparation, with grace before meals'. 'It is not a Eucharist, but rather a special meal, to which we all look forward, which includes a bottle of wine . . . we normally begin (in winter) by lighting the table candles and singing the very early Christian hymn, "Hail, gladdening light".' Prayers follow from all and at the close there is a verse from another eucharistic hymn. 'I then cut a slice from the loaf and pour out a glass of wine, both of which we pass round, ending with a salutation, or the grace, and a joining of hands.' This moving picture of family festivity and worship is described in *The New Reformation*, pp. 84–5. Here too, though without the sombreness, is the spirit of '*ce qu'a fait le Christ à la derniere Cène*'. I much regret that John Robinson's *Exploration into God* appeared too late in 1967 to be considered alongside his other works. If this spiritual autobiography can be summarized in a sentence it represents a movement away from van Buren towards Tillich, away from the avidities of logical positivism and towards an existentialist and personalist faith.

3 *The Times*, 3 January 1967.

4 *Planning the Ecumenical Parish*, published at 23 Linden Road, Northampton.